The Career
As a Path
To the SOUL

Stories and Thoughts about
Finding Meaning in Work and Life

DAVID ROTTMAN

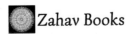 Zahav Books

Cover art: Quasicrystal III Illustrations © Eric J. Heller 2013

Cover Design by Maayan Laufer

Printed in the United States of America

ISBN-13: 9781935184485

Library of Congress Control Number: 2013936704

Published by Zahav Books Inc.   New York, New York

Contact: info@zahavbooks.com

In Honor of the Life and Work of Dr. Yoram Kaufmann

Psychologist, Teacher, Author, Mentor, and Great Soul

-Contents-

- To the Reader-

One of the most wonderful and yet troublesome human impulses is the desire to live with a sense of serving a higher purpose. In fact, the definition I like the most for a "path to the soul" is *a way of living in meaningful connection to something greater than our bounded sense of ourselves.*

This desire is a fierce and relentless craving in some people and yet it's barely noticed by others. When the need for personal meaning makes a strong and dramatic appearance in a person's life, we can often see that this wonderful impulse is paradoxically the beginning of a trouble-filled sequence of events because the specific nature of our own very personal higher purpose is rarely "given" in life, usually it must be discovered and often with a great deal of effort and pain.

I wrote the stories in this book and put together the accompanying thoughts to illustrate a few of the ways a path to the soul can be achieved through a special kind of work, work on oneself. This is certainly not the only way a higher purpose can make entry into a person's life, but it is perhaps the most <u>reliable</u> way for those craving meaning. Working on oneself is what we can do instead of wishing and hoping and waiting for that meaningful connection—that otherwise may never come.

Just a few introductory remarks are in order to set the stage for the stories. First, what is "something greater?" When a person gets the sense they have received an "assignment" in life to do something specific that is important, there are usually gratifying feelings that accompany this task, particularly the reassuring feeling of certainty. When genuine and real, this assignment usually carries a powerful conviction that it comes from a place within that is more encompassing and grander than our everyday consciousness and our familiar sense of our self. The assignment is experienced as inherently of great worth and produces feelings of fundamental satisfaction with life.

This inspiring place within is the potential source for a life-changing realization about what it means to be human and to be alive. Think of it: something tangible and valid exists <u>inside</u> of us and it can give us a crucial task or assignment in life! The experience of connecting to this kind of highly personal meaning is one of those stark defining markers by which people come to measure their lives; everything is either "before" or "after" it. A convincing experience of this kind—that something greater exists within and that it comes with a sense of direction—infallibly alters the trajectory of a person's life.

Of course there are innumerable erroneous and "false" voices that contain misleading messages about our true direction in life, and how are we to know the difference? ("I would like to do something important with my life," many people say. "I want a career that's meaningful… if only I could know for certain how to get it.") This dilemma is illustrated in the very first story. One of the markers of the genuineness of a "higher" assignment is that it is a renewable personal asset that is unshakable, permanent and lasting. Another marker of the genuineness of the assignment is if it comes without humbug or pretension or grandstanding. The feeling of relating to something greater isn't aggrandizing, just the opposite.

The place of origin where we connect to something "greater" than ourselves can also be experienced as coming from the <u>outside</u>, through the challenge of honoring the requirements we encounter in our profession: the sacred premise or "antique soul" of our profession. (See Chapter Eight) This challenge can sometimes take all our personal resources, all we've got of integrity and courage and the desire to honor our own values.

Whether originating from without or within, finding one's own path can most reliably be achieved, for those who lack it, through that special kind of work on oneself that is illustrated in a variety of ways in the stories. This work--to raise our own level of conscious functioning--can be compared to a series of locks that raise a ship to a higher level on a river. The work to raise awareness of the specific dimensions of our own nature is like the special kind of work that goes on within the fixed chamber of a river lock. Bounded on either side by gates, a ship going through this process is immobile. Nothing progressive and forward-moving seems to be happening while the lock chamber is filling up. It might seem to someone who had never seen the process before that the ship is permanently stuck. This could lead to confusion and dismay.

But in fact a lot of important and purposeful work is going on. Gears are being rotated, valves are being opened and shut, gates are being drawn open and closed watertight in sequence, and when ready, the water from upstream rushes in. When the level in the chamber is high enough, the gate opens and the ship moves forward only a small distance and the next lock is ready for its work. That small distance is actually great progress. When the upper gate of the last lock is opened, the ship is ready to launch freely onto a new and higher plane of navigation. A new gradient of forward movement has been achieved.

While the time it takes to "turn" a ship's lock is often short, the work of raising the gradient of one's basic conscious functioning can have differing durations, short or long, and it can sometimes become the primary and exclusive focus of a person's life because nothing can go forward without it, and because as previously mentioned not many of us start out with the wonderful blessing of a long-lasting connection to a higher purpose. The analogy to the ship's lock is helpful because once again, to someone who has never seen the process before, certain aspects and stages of the work on oneself do have an apparent lack of forward movement. That work can be mistaken for stagnation. One of the contributions of the stories in this book is that they show in detail how much work is actually going on during these "raising the level" stages, and how these private but often mighty efforts create a new and productive way forward.

It's really a startling perspective when you think about it: the lack of a connection to a higher purpose is often where those fierce and intractable lifelong problems begin--and these are not exotic or unheard of kinds of problems. For many people nothing can go forward and nothing can go right without a connection to their individual purpose, and so as a result real troubles occur in jobs and career, money, relationships, love, and health. Even the feeling that life is worth living becomes degraded when there is no connection to a path forward. It's likely that every bitter person can be understood as one who has missed that connection to a higher purpose.

The process of working toward an individual path to the soul is entirely different for each person but has the universal benefit of making anyone who undertakes it a more complete person. (The goal is important as a guiding idea but the more important thing is the work done along the way.) Completeness means doing not only all the usual things we do in life but also adding on a new dimension--relating to a higher purpose—a process that rounds us out, enabling us to fill our "intended" shape. This leads to living on a daily basis with that famously desirable feeling of "living the life I was meant to live" and "being the person I was meant to be." For many people the sense of being on one's own path has to come from digging into the material of one's own life until a personal purpose makes itself known. That alone is convincing.

Once we have some idea of our very own higher purpose we are immediately presented with the requirement that we serve it. The attitude of being in service to a higher purpose is a key component of direction and meaning and fulfillment, and can bring a sense of adventure and excitement to life. (But not always those last two. As we will see in Chapter Four even tragedy can be a path to the soul.) When, for whatever reason, we have nothing greater to serve in life, chaotic and painful feelings fill the vacuum along with disappointment, anxiety and meaninglessness.

Serving something that we sense is greater than our conscious awareness, leads to some controversial implications. For example, from this point of view not all serious problems in work and life arise from a "pathological" origin. Everyone knows that problems arising from difficult experiences in childhood are crucial to uncover. The cause and effect of these experiences can never be underestimated. But even so these troubles from the past comprise less than a total picture of what is going on in a human being. Many problems also arise as a goad or a prod to raise our awareness to a sense of what life assignment—and what meaning—we need to serve. This is a task for adults, a task worthy of the whole person and a whole life.

But a caution is in order. Even though much of this book is devoted to the idea that problems can arise for the sake of inciting or provoking or (more gently) leading a person to become a more complete and more conscious person, I want to set a boundary limit on that idea right away. We rightly ask: What about the visitation of terrible problems, problems that create enormous suffering? It offends our sense of mercy and justice to think that all undeserved pain is nevertheless really just an impetus for greater consciousness. We have to differentiate those human problems that are undeserved and simply must be endured, from problems that have a goal and purpose hidden behind them. In other words, we have to be able to distinguish between burdens that must be carried as part of the full measure of the human condition, and burdens that are indications of a need for forward movement in the direction of a goal arising from within us. That is sometimes very difficult to differentiate: is this a problem pushing me higher or is this a problem I must simply carry as part of my fate? And to complicate matters even more, the two are sometimes halves of the same coin, as we see especially vividly in the last three stories.

Keeping that boundary limit in mind, the "serving something greater" perspective shows us that many problems can never be solved on their own terms; they can only be solved at the level of connection to our higher purpose. The Swiss psychologist C.G. Jung made the striking statement that the great and important problems of life can never be solved on their own terms but only outgrown. It is a normal and non-pathological state of affairs in human life to need to "outgrow" oneself in order to reach a potential that wants to be lived.

If a person wants and needs to find their personal meaning and higher purpose, there will be times when psychological courage will be tested. There are no previously existing guidelines on how to achieve a path to the soul. It's always a voyage of discovery into the unknown, with mystery as a backdrop, although certainty is a legitimate goal.

A path to the soul is in fact a view forward to a goal. A path to the soul gives a direction that points to how and where further development needs to take place and where there is a promise of a more creative way of living. Asking about the nature of the path, and its goal, is the first step in constructing a path to the soul.

Stories

-Prologue-
Fireworks in a Therapist's Office

In my sunny South-facing office in the middle of Manhattan, I have a wonderful example of how inventive and resourceful a human being can be, when challenged to live creatively. This marvel is a full-size replica of one of the last works of Matisse, from the final phase of his life when he was confined mostly to his bed. Unable to stand and paint, he was propped up with pillows, and used a scissors to cut out colored paper, which was then pinned to a background by an assistant, according to Matisse's direction.

My patients sit on a generously wide pumpkin-colored velour couch with three pillows: one firebrick red, one chartreuse, and one cadet blue. Above this couch, in a large gold frame, facing me, there is that poster by Matisse called "Nuit De Noel," originally a gouache-painted collage of cut and pasted paper. Panels of bright purple, orange and green representing the fireworks explode over the dark blue sky above Nice on Christmas night. At the top, a burst of yellow color spreads out its fingers underneath a canopy of white and black stars. Like fireworks that remain in the mind's eye, I can see this work even when not looking at it, the white and black stars trailing after a huge yellow star that explodes into the mysterious blue sky. Matisse covered the walls of his room with these arabesques of color. Surrounded by this work, he said in his last days, "I am never alone."

The awe that fireworks produce is a reminder to me of a very special awe that commands to be felt when we witness the miracle of transformation in a human being. Then and there is a testament to the fact when a man or woman's deepest psychic images are met with acceptance and understanding, a burst of new energy explodes and starts to become real. Those fireworks within the human soul are as visible to the observing eye as anything in the outer world.

Bursts of light of this kind do not quickly fade into the night as with fireworks. Instead their impact within the psyche remains. Their illumination lights up what is inside a person and reveals what formerly lived in darkness.

-Chapter One-
"I Need The Job That Is Absolutely Right For Me"

How do we find certainty in this life? Is it possible that certainty lives in some mysterious realm of its own, waiting for us to make contact? The story that follows is about a young man who is "completely lost" but nevertheless wants to find the job that is "absolutely right for me." He learns that the path to finding such a job involves participating in a process of "creating himself," a strange expression, and a challenging idea for sure.

On the day that he would mark as the "real" beginning of his life, Ron Halmon was sitting with several of his friends and roommates around the television. It was a rainy Sunday afternoon in the middle of November on the upper West Side of Manhattan. The walls on their pre-war apartment were peeling paint, and the high ceiling was damp from four days of unending rain. The huge old television, propped up at an odd angle on a roller cart from the corner appliance store, had been moved into the middle of the living room. Ron and his friends were

3

watching a football game of only mild interest, in the middle of the season with nothing at stake.

For weeks Ron had been anxiously casting about for a new direction in his career. He had been laid off as a customer service representative--a "glorified complaint handler" as he put it--from a hotel chain. The combination of his savings and his unemployment checks was going to run out soon.

This was the second job he been laid off from in six months, and the eighth job he had held in the five years since college. He was twenty-seven and his career was, in his words, "in the toilet."

While he was watching the game, Ron was also trading desultory comments with his friends on many topics including football, commercials, politics, war, the origins of rock and roll, and the state of the economy. A tone of frustration and irritation, along with a certain amount of resignation, was there to hear in all his sarcastic comments about "what doctors recommend most," and "football is a game played between the ears," and "the golden era of doo-wop will never die." More than anything else, Ron's comments sounded gloomy. Although to him no one seemed to notice, Ron was doing a lot of suffering. As he would discover later, his friends were quite aware that there was an ominous sense of a crisis building in his life.

This was despite the fact that he had a ready smile, and was handsome by his girlfriends' accounts: he was tall and thin, with jet black hair and blue eyes. But when one of his girlfriends, an artist, painted his portrait she chose a gloomy glance, looking downward, that perfectly captured his most frequent private expression. After she gave him the finished portrait, he turned it to the wall. Later he put it in a closet.

Halftime came in the game and still another commercial came on, this one for the local chapter of a national charity. It showed a famous former athlete in the rehabilitation room of a local hospital, helping an adult patient walk between a set of parallel bars. Later in the same commercial the athlete, now showing himself at work in his new career, was in a small pool, helping a grateful child to float on his back. It was a commercial Ron and his friends had watched before many times.

"That's it," Ron said. In the midst of the ongoing conversation, no one paid him any attention.

At first, it might have seemed as if Ron himself hadn't really said anything. The statement seemed to come from another place in his being, a place deeper and with more resonance than the place of comments about television. Something in his being had been touched, struck.

"That's physical therapy, isn't it?" he said aloud, again as if to himself.

"Yeah, and rehabilitation," said one of his friends.

"That's it," Ron said again. "That's what I'm going to do with my life."

"Yeah, sure," said one of his friends.

"How do you get to do that?" said Ron. "You've got to get a degree, right?"

"Sure, you're going to be a physical therapist," said the friend. "And I'm going to be an astronaut."

"No, I can do this," said Ron. "The kids would love me. I can feel it," he said.

On Monday Ron called his local hospital and asked for the physical therapy department. After several run-arounds, he found someone willing to tell him what was required: "P/T requires a three-year academic and practical matriculation, along with a 26 week internship." The very words sounded frightening to Ron, but he swallowed his feelings and vowed to do something more the next day.

On Tuesday, Ron found there was a nearby university with a program in physical therapy, just a subway ride away. He made an appointment with the admissions director, who handed Ron a thick embossed blue and white application packet filled with forms, and suggested that he might like to sit in that very morning on a class.

Without any warning Ron found himself sitting in the back of a shiny modern classroom crowded with younger students with laptops and notepads. The instructor walked in and quietly wrote the topic on the board, "Organic Chemistry and Its Role in the Body's Metabolism." As if turning on a machine, the instructor began to speak in a monotone about chemical chains, enzymes, and reactions. The students made notes frantically as the list of terms and concepts piled up faster and faster.

By the end of the 50 minute lecture, Ron was in tears. He had never been a good student in science, most of his grades in all subjects had been mediocre, and he was crushed by the realization that this would stand as an immovable obstacle in the path of what seemed like his true and proper career.

He went home in a state of morbid discouragement and lay on his bed for hours, as he had done many times in the past. One of his friends sat on the edge of Ron's bed and said "Listen, Ron, get your ass in gear, go down to the unemployment office and take whatever they've got." The implication was clear: his friends didn't think Ron could make it as a physical therapist, any more than he did.

People like Ron who are plagued by doubts about what is right for them are the very people who often express a need for a strange and remarkable thing called Absolute Knowledge. As Ron put it, he wanted to find the one career that is "absolutely right for me."

The very idea of Absolute Knowledge of oneself sends a cold wave of fear, a belly chill, into many other people. The questions raised by Absolute Knowledge (if there is such a thing, it might have terrible implications!) can be deeply unsettling. The topic has been known to set off tension and even rage in some people.

Absolute Knowledge could be defined as the strange occurrences that manifest when the psyche knows something outside of the limits and boundaries of space and time. The term is usually invoked when seemingly "paranormal" events occur, such as telepathic events or events seeming to give accurate foreknowledge.

But there is another dimension of Absolute Knowledge that is more close to home. In these cases our total psyche knows the facts of the situation even if we ourselves in our limited consciousness don't know. This powerful and awe-inspiring experience can be summarized as

"Something in me knows, even if I myself do not."

Why was this necessary, and what made it arise? Ron was unlike the segment of the population who come to their true career interests in an undisturbed way in adolescence or early adulthood. (He had several friends who could not "relate" to his dilemma; one friend had wanted to be a physician "as long as he could remember," the other was certain of a career as a musician when he was just seven years old.) Ron was also unlike those who go to sleep permanently in a profession that is nevertheless wrong for them. Instead he was searching for an extraordinary inner voice, the voice of certainty, that would state unequivocally and with great power "You Should Do THIS."

Ron and people like him have a conviction, which they might even be able to express in a way, that somewhere in their being, somewhere deep and therefore inaccessible, the right career is known, absolutely and very concretely. While this was what Ron was seeking, again for many people those inaccessible depths are a stomach-chilling experience that is better off avoided.

Since he was certain of only what was missing, Ron's constant pain was that at the level of consciousness, at the level of his everyday normal awareness, the "it" (his true career) was not known. It hadn't been "revealed" as it were. Ron wanted to be spoken to by this place in himself, this place where deep certainty and truth come from, much as ancient prophets were spoken to in momentous revelations. Anything short of this power of truth would mean his life would continue without fulfillment, that he was consigned to a miserably unhappy fate.

It was sad that a connection with the source of inner knowledge and certainty seemed so remote to him. Ron spent long hours "tramping" in all weather through the Rambles of Central Park, or just sitting on a rock in the park, waiting to be "hit" by what he should do with himself. The waiting seemed to be interminable, it was an endless trial.

During this time Ron could not accept that this source of inner knowledge couldn't be called up and contacted at will. (He often dreamt of telephone calls that couldn't get through.) During his teens and twenties, he thought it was the fault of his problems with will power. He often thought that words of will power could be magical. "Focus," "determination," "execution," "passion," "drive," "desire," and "vision." He pasted note cards with these words to his computer, and he carried them in his wallet. He had an extensive library of self-help books whose basic message was "Where there's a will, there's a way."

"Not for me," Ron finally concluded. He had an aching sense of something missing, and like many others in his generation, his career had been one of extended floundering. The pattern was a familiar one: different jobs usually of short duration in different fields, temp work, periods of unemployment, feelings of being useless, aimless, wandering about. A sense of being out of the mainstream of life.

And like most people who flounder, Ron had "heard" other voices, voices seeming at first to carry absolute self-knowledge, but which had played tricksterish jokes on him.

"It's screenwriting," said an inner voice of authority, on one occasion when Ron was just out of college. Ron started but didn't finish three different scripts.

At another time the voice said "It's designing web pages." Ron tried his hand at this new idea and after investing money and time, the old disappointment started to creep in.

When things didn't go right, when as he put it he "crashed and burned," then in effect he went back to the voice, to the place where Absolute Knowledge of himself seemed to come from, and he looked for some reassurance and renewed inspiration and a helping hand. And this is what he heard: "Screenwriting? You? That's ridiculous. Come back down to earth, you nincompoop."

Each time it had been an illusion. That wasn't the "real" voice talking, it was an impostor. He hadn't made real contact with his soul. The inner certainty that first came about screenwriting or web page design was a gross deception. The experience of being fooled only made Ron trust himself even less, and added to his despair.

After these experiences had accumulated a collective weight, Ron was so disoriented and confused that he had the feeling that if the inner certainty finally and actually did come, he might think it was still another trick. He might miss out even then, which would be a kind of final irony. At the ripe old age of twenty-seven, a cranky gloominess had settled into his being, in a dangerously habitual way.

Other people, mostly Ron's friends, told him that the cure for his lack of certainty would be to pick one of the career options, and follow it up to the end. They told him to persist past the doubts and uncertainties, to keep on with the screenwriting or web page design or the start-up ideas, to get past the initial disappointment and the let-downs, and to see what developed when he put the doubts in their place, or laid them aside.

It might have been a solution. It would have meant not waiting for the Absolute Knowledge, not waiting for the upsurge of true certainty, but plunging ahead instead into the world of work with exactly the sense that "this one is the only possible career, the only possible job."

It would have meant learning to keep the trickster voices at bay, learning to function effectively even when plagued by doubts and inner voices of uncertainty. This would have been a task of utmost importance, so important that it might have been more important than having a sense of absolute rightness about the career. To proceed in spite of doubts is an ethical achievement of the personality that is profoundly important.

But in Ron's case, this solution was sterile. He had applied all of his available discipline to his jobs and still he felt cheated, disappointed, and lacking in direction. Worst of all, he felt helpless.

In his despair, he took a referral from a family friend to meet with me. Having reached the bottom of despair, he came without the desire to escape, which most people naturally and understandably, have about the process of working with themselves as the material. He came without the sense that anything else might work for him. Without knowing it yet, he had arrived at the threshold of the realm of Absolute Knowledge, from which he would build a meaningful life and career.

"I have no more hope," said Ron in his first session. "If this can't help me, I don't have anything else to try."

"What led you to this?" I asked.

"It's a crash and burn story," Ron said. "I'll tell it to you, but I'm not sure how much good that will do." While he talked, he built a fort around himself on the couch, using the three pillows. "Ok, ok," he said. "Let's get going."

For many sessions that followed, Ron explored the ways in which his career, and his life, had followed wrong turns. It was a relief to him to be able to pour out the "gory details" of jobs where he had been let go, of opportunities squandered, of impermanent moments filled with promise and joy and relief that then led to defeats, some passing and some crushing.

In many sessions he cried, while in others he pounded his hand and fist together in frustration and anger. As he said, there always seemed to be more--more and more episodes of failure and loss that he had nearly forgotten and now could add to the growing list. He often spoke of how much shame he felt over each episode. The cake from a celebration when he landed a job had once not been finished before he had been let go. The half empty box in the refrigerator reminded him of many painful things.

The scope of this painful "life review" widened. Crash and burn stories were not just about his career, but also his girlfriends, his money situation, even his health. Meanwhile, to make ends meet Ron took a temporary job as a "customer representative" at a department store. After a number of months had passed, he looked up from his usual downward glance, and said in a session, "You know, I think I'm ready to ask a new question."

"What's that?" I asked.

"How can I get where I need to go? It seems so obvious, and that's what I came here for in the first place, but now I'm ready to ask the question for real. How do I start?"

"How would you describe your situation now?"

"I don't know. I'm still just lost."

"Do your best to make a picture of it, what does it look like?"

"It's like I suddenly woke up to find myself in the middle of the desert and there's nothing around me but sand. I have no idea which direction to take, no idea how to get back to civilization. I haven't got a compass. There aren't any tracks leading to where I am now."

"Go on."

"I have no idea where to start walking, but I know that the only important thing is that I've got to get going, just start going. If I don't, I'll just die. But I'm stuck. I don't know which way to go." There was a pause. Ron was tense, and the pain on his face was severe.

"Let's assume there might be several ways you could go," I said. "That is, presuming you don't have the voice of inner certainty that says `Walk that way, there is your best direction.'"

Ron smiled but just for a moment.

"So what else could you try?" I continued. "Put yourself into it."

"Well, I could simply pick a direction and keep walking straight until I couldn't go on," said Ron. "But I feel like I've already tried that in my life, and it didn't work."

"Then what else?"

"I could walk half as far I could go, in one straight line, and then walk all the way back to the starting point. That wouldn't accomplish much, probably. I would just be retracing my path."

Ron grimaced. He was concentrating very hard on this highly unusual exercise. "I'm starting to feel stuck again. I feel like I need some help."

"What other ways could you walk?"

"I could walk around in circles like a madman," he said. It came explosively, with all the pain of what he had been living. As he said it, I saw fireworks burst in the sky, and I could feel the transformation process was alive in the room.

"Yes." There was a long pause. "Could you walk around those circles to explore?" I asked.

"What do you mean?" he asked.

"Let's say you walked around in ever larger spirals, with your starting place as the center. That way you would explore ever larger parts of the terrain, in a systematic way."

"Yes," said Ron, "that would be an option. But I still might not discover anything."

"You would have to make discoveries. You would get some idea of where your starting point was, how it related to the surrounding environment. You would become an expert of a kind on your starting area, on your habitat."

Ron was thoughtful for a while and then he laughed. "I'm smart enough to know we're not just talking about the desert. How does this relate to anything in my life?"

"For many sessions now we've been spiraling around the story of what's happened to you, about the patterns of your life, and your feelings of being lost."

"Ok."

"And now it's time to begin evaluating the terrain. What discoveries have you made?"

"Well, like you said I do seem to have some patterns. I get fooled by my mistakes, then I crash and burn."

"Any others?"

"I can't think of any."

"How about a discovery, something essential, that is positive about you?"

Surprisingly, Ron didn't hesitate.

"I know I have something I want to give. I want to be able to help people, I want to do something that matters."

"Yes. That's you, isn't it?"

Ron look surprised for a moment and then burst into tears, and sobbed for many long minutes.

Here he had reached the same Absolute Knowledge that had come to him while watching the TV commercial, but now he was on a different loop of the spiral. Now he had something, a spiral-woven net, a net of that miraculous substance we call consciousness, with which to "catch" the Absolute Knowledge and hold on to it. He was beginning to get an objective sense of himself, the beginnings of a center from which to act. The mystery of transformation was at work. The healing power of the psyche, and its illuminating light, were at work.

In his sessions Ron returned again and again to the "facts" about himself that he had discovered in the middle of his "desert." In each session he would begin with the negative pole, all the "baggage" of things that had gone wrong, and then he would circle around to the positive pole, the things about him that were true but also "good." The fact that he had "something to give" gradually became an anchor for this pole.

When enough time had passed (it was the time of his own rate of change, never to be compared to anyone else) Ron said our work of "drastic inner reconstruction" had led him to try to express how he felt in another descriptive image. He was no longer lost in that desert. Now he was lost in a forest. There were trees and birds and animals, and a stream with flowing water, he said. And it was not far from a town, because he could smell foods cooking and hear the sounds of human voices.

At this point the change in Ron was great enough to have an impact on his career. After some hesitation he called the same admissions director and asked for a new application for the physical therapy program. The heavy packet seemed even heavier. Fearful that his old ways might return, he decided to test himself by once again sitting in on several scientific and technical courses, as a non-matriculated student. This time the experience was different.

"At first I was really scared," he reported later. "I wanted to run out of the class. But then I remembered I know how to circle around at least some of my fears. I tried it while I was sitting there. I had to tune out of the lecture for a while and I started walking around my fears in my mind. You know, all the questions we talked about...where did my fears begin, how have they changed, when do they come up. Then I realized I was already back listening to the lecture. All the bad feelings lost their hold on me after I started spiraling! You can't believe how excited I got. I sat there and I was just really excited."

In the midst of these new developments and his understandable elation, Ron had not lost track of his difficulties:

"I don't have any illusions," he said. "I know it's going to be hard. I know I'll have the impulse to run out of the classes again. I'm resigned to that. But while I was sitting there I realized I'm going to be able to study this stuff because I'm interested in it. I mean, there's a lot there to get interested in, you know?" He paused and built the fort again with the three pillows. "I don't have to do things by will power any more. That's an incredible relief."

Ron now engaged in the process of proving himself to be correct. He undertook the physical therapy training and maintained a B average. The work proved to be as difficult as he anticipated and he was compelled to arrange for a private tutor. His feelings of being "lost" and "in a madman's panic" arose whenever a major exam or paper was due, and he still had occasional bouts of gloom to contend with, but nevertheless he completed all the requirements. Along with this dimension of his life, there was the new dimension of "continuous revelations" as he put it. His encounter with himself became a habit, a way of living, with continuous discoveries.

After graduation he found work immediately in a hospital rehabilitation unit.

"Do I think I should celebrate?" he asked.

"What do you think?"

"It's a risk," Ron said. He thought about it. "No, it would have been a risk before." His voice was firm. "Now it's a time for celebration."

Ron invited all his friends to a picnic near the Bethesda Foundation in Central Park, a fitting location. The Pool of Bethesda was known in biblical times as a place of disgrace and shame as well as healing. It was where he had often gone during the "lost years." The party was a memorable success with the highlight a dance in a circle, so joyous it was even joined by passers-by.

We met on the morning before his first day on the job. Summing up, Ron said "I had to learn to walk in life, as if I'd never walked before."

"I'm sure that will help with your patients," I said. There was no need to explain.

Years have passed since then, and Ron continues to be gripped by his involvement with his work. He has been promoted, and now trains others. And as he predicted, the children love him.

Driven by his search for "Absolute Knowledge," Ron experienced nothing less than the birth of his adult personality and his essential life vitality, through creating a new set of images.

This new level of vitality, the capacity for passionate living, was the reliable, indeed infallible resource that he needed to replace blind will power, which had always let him down at crucial moments. Like many others before him, he had tried to use will power to obliterate his doubts; now he learned the proper use of will power to engage and encounter his doubts.

Ron had been an inadequately created person as a whole. That was his "desert." (His first dream at the beginning of our work together was that he was marching in a protest, carrying a sign. When he looked up he saw the sign was blank.) Among other things, he had been a person with an inadequate conception of life and of what was possible for him. He was not a fact to himself.

His desire and ability to contribute to the world through his work was only a tentative hypothesis in the beginning. Like many people who are "lost" in their careers, the very idea of a "meaningful career" was an obscure, foreign and alienating concept for him--it seemed hostile, a cruel joke, as well as remote and unreal. By contrast, his gloom seemed much more "evidence based" i.e. more real.

His unknown fears were so great, and his ability to turn them into known fears was so poorly developed, that he was literally moved out of his seat by fear in the classroom before he could register what had happened.

Therefore before his true career could come into being, he needed to enlarge and amplify himself so that his own reactions and needs could become intelligible and livable, and could appear in a positive light.

He arrived at his first-ever connection to a new vitality through a special kind of circumambulation; his spiral-like review of his life gave

15

him a sense of creating something with himself as the material. He discovered that even under the most limited of circumstances, even alone in the desert he could make a new kind of pattern with his life.

But how could this be so? Not just for Ron but for anyone: how is it that a lost person can find their way?

Just as a spider has the structure of the web inside itself, so to speak, before it begins spinning, so Ron had his meaning and his vitality within himself in a latent form, in those untapped images that came out in our work together. But he had been chronically unable to find something right for himself because he had no center, because he had never learned anything of his own terrain, of his own dimensions. Unlike the spider who, we presume, doesn't reflect on the design of the web, Ron needed to be both an active and a reflective participant in his own task of "person design."

Ron's story illustrates the fact that people with a need for the Absolute Knowledge of what is the right career, and what is the right way to live, need to be "spinning," working on the problem in a middle sort of a way, not just standing still on the one hand, and not giving up on their need for the Absolute Knowledge either.

By going back and forth from the negative pole to the positive pole, from hopelessness to hope and back again, from images of gloom to glimpses of fulfillment, he was circumambulating around a center. In that center he was creating a new premise, a new organization of the self. Ron story's illustrates the fact that people who are lost in their lives or careers need to walk around their problem by picturing it, describing it, amplifying it, giving it attention, energy, and even devotion. Uncovering what is hidden or lost in a life involves circling repeatedly around an unknown, starting with the chaotic beginning, until the unknown becomes visible and knowable in the form of an image.

As the great psychologist C.G. Jung pointed out, there is a chicken and egg question of whether this center is created by consciousness, and by this spiral work, or whether the center is pre-existing and attracts consciousness like a magnet. When we devote energy and care to finding out something of great importance, it is as if we stimulate the Absolute

Knowledge in its own realm and it reaches out to meet us halfway, as it were. In its own realm this knowledge is detached from consciousness and is self subsistent--it exists even though it is not known by anyone. Yet despite its self subsistence it is responsive to the right kind of precisely attuned attention from human beings. Once again, it is as if Absolute Knowledge was waiting… waiting for a human being and just the right conditions to move into another realm, the realm of human action.

So Ron needed to take up the problem of finding the right career but in an indirect way. This meant temporarily sacrificing the pursuit of his immediate goal, a meaningful job, for the pursuit of self-understanding and self-acceptance. The far-off goal of finding the right job needed to be sacrificed for a goal more in the present moment. It took a great deal of courage to commit himself to this more pressing goal of finding a right way of experiencing himself in the here and now, a way of living in the present. That consisted of pouring his energy into exploring himself just for his own sake, and then experiencing the pleasure and satisfaction that resulted.

Once he could "catch" the passion and the pleasure of exploring his interests, and the intense satisfaction of experiencing himself structuring his world, then he was on his way. Gradually and slowly he built up this new core of himself until both he and the right career could come into being. Since the right career is always a blend of the "rightness" of the person and the "rightness" of the job, neither can be left out of the equation.

These exploratory tasks were where Ron needed to apply himself by submitting to their necessity. In effect he learned a new set of skills. He made a very creative use of his imagination to make images of his predicament; these images were his alone and were the indispensable material for building his "view" of himself. He used his memory and his mind first to make the painful life review of his troubled life. He made use of the passion of his whole being, his deepest emotions, to suffer knowingly and willingly the consequences of what he had done to himself previously, unknowingly and unwillingly. Then finally he was willing to take his insights to another level: only when he had made enough progress within was he ready to put himself through the outer tests. The insights needed to be tested through action and then applied with perseverance.

The broad implications of Ron's story are nothing less than astonishing. Ron started with very limited life and career energies: his sense of direction was virtually non-existent. That was the state of his "found" or "given" world; that had been his fate. The baseline energies of his personality were simply unsuitable for a decent life. By concentrating even those limited energies on himself, the astonishing result was a great upsurge in available energy, a truly remarkable enlarging and widening of his personality. Ron raised the baseline level of his essential life energy and passion, to a point that could he express through daily living.

Ron's story shows that human beings do not have a closed psychic system. When a new pattern is woven into the psyche, a remarkable release of energy can occur. Through the right means, often with painstaking effort, and with the proper attitude, people like Ron can participate in the creation of an immense shift in their life and career energies. Those who, like Ron, are not fortunate enough to have been born with a high or even a satisfactory level of life and career meaning may, if conditions are right, nevertheless achieve experiences of such "cosmic" import that Absolute Knowledge becomes real and tangible, along with a discernible release of energy for creative living. Can it really be so? The skeptics among Ron's friends were the last to be convinced, but even they came around.

In Ron's momentous realization in the classroom we can actually observe what Absolute Knowledge looks like in the specific form of a human being, in "Ron" form. At such moments true revelations become accessible at a very human and personal level. It was crucial for Ron to realize that working on himself was the essential thing in finding the right career. This allowed his Absolute Knowledge to come out of the realm of the Absolute and enter into life in real and concrete form.

Finally, couldn't this story be seen as a simple account of a young man who is troubled, comes to therapy and unburdens himself, and as a result gets on his way in life? Surely there are many such stories?

In this very specific case, it was more than the right career that Ron was seeking. It was also the deeply meaningful experience that something on the outside can mirror something on the inside. This sense of unity, a unity of something important inside melding into a very specific outer form, such as an occupation, is a stupendously meaningful experience. The feeling of living out such a connection is profoundly touching, producing feelings of healing emotion. Living in the center of a feeling of such "rightness" is--beyond all words used to describe it--an emotionally satisfying feeling. It means living with a sense one is on a level beyond the need for belief or non-belief. The "unity experience" is another way of describing the promise of Absolute Knowledge, a realm where we can experience something "transcendent," the oneness of inner and outer, the soul and the world.

DAVID ROTTMAN

-Chapter Two-
"I've Grokked That I'm A Force Field"
How rage is a creative act that is blocked

This is the story of a man who was confronted with the need to find a creative way to respond to a tyrannical new boss—and that forced him to look within himself for the first time. There he was surprised to find the great and awesome power of transformation in the human psyche, as if the whole experience had a hidden goal.

When his violent fantasies about his boss began to return again and again to grisly scenes of death and murder, Mark Wilpon realized that it would be a good idea for him to get some help.

While driving home from work or taking a shower, Mark found himself envisioning gory scenes in which Hal, his boss, was torn apart by wild animals (usually hyenas but sometimes lions) or was slowly run over by a huge truck with enormous crushing wheels. Much more disturbingly, Mark also had fantasies of slowly choking the life from his boss with his own hands.

Mark's idea of himself as basically a "good person" had been tarnished by these recurring fantasies. He derived an undeniable gruesome satisfaction from the slowly unfolding repetitious details of Hal "getting his due." But Mark didn't like the fact that he couldn't control the fantasies; they distracted him from listening to others, even at home. He wondered if this all meant there was a flaw in his character that was more serious than he would have expected.

All the problems at work had begun two years previously when Hal Smith became Mark's boss in the programming department at their large manufacturing company just outside Philadelphia. Their relationship started off on the wrong foot and deteriorated progressively. In Mark's version of things, Hal had criticized Mark's work with increasing bluntness, and had begun to hand out "plum" assignments to other less-qualified co-workers.

What upset Mark the most was that Hal embarrassed him with derogatory comments. At meetings with co-workers and suppliers, and in front of Mark's own staff, Hal frequently made cutting remarks. Mark found the embarrassment excruciating. It was simply unbearable. These scenes in which he endured embarrassment at Hal's hands replayed themselves in his mind again and again, only to be followed by the repeating fantasies of Hal undergoing grinding torture. The ever more violent thoughts of revenge were now torturing Mark in turn.

During this time Mark developed what his physician described as a "pre-ulcer." He started taking acid inhibitors and was also taking a number of other medications for several different conditions including high blood pressure. He had developed night sweats, a condition in which he sometimes awoke in the middle of the night to find his bed sheets soaking wet with perspiration. He had also gained weight and had stopped working out in the small gym he had built in his basement.

Prior to Hal's arrival on the scene, Mark's career had been "remarkably successful," in his own view. After attending a state university on the West Coast, Mark had been accepted into an entry-level position with the company as a data-entry clerk in their Florida subsidiary. He had taken many of the opportunities for training that the company offered, had accepted transfers, and over the course of the years he had progressed to his current position as a supervisor of forty programmers at a beautiful new suburban executive park. The increases in his salary had enabled him to take out a 30-year mortgage on a house in the suburbs and to raise a family.

Mark was a large heavy-boned man with a broad balding forehead. He had a soft way of talking and a quiet laugh. He was a science fiction buff and his black satchel briefcase usually was stuffed with thick paperbacks whose covers showed intergalactic travelers or space/time warriors.

His distinguishing feature besides his size was his large but well-trimmed sandy-brown mustache. He dressed neatly, preferring dark green or tan suits, and on Fridays he wore red socks, a source of never-ending jokes with his fellow employees. He had a warm and familiar way with the people who worked for him, and was a favorite boss for the programmers, some of whom had worked for him for years. His record of trouble-free management of his area had been noted many times by the company's yearly audits of absenteeism and employee complaints.

Mark's physician asked if he was under any new stress on the job. When Mark raised his voice and said that he had a violent antipathy to his boss, the physician gave him my card. In his first session with me, his first session ever of any kind of therapy, Mark described the angry fantasies that were troubling him and outlined the history of his relationship with Hal.

"I didn't know what to expect when Hal took over but I was willing to give him the benefit of the doubt," Mark said. "I pride myself on trying to keep an open mind."

Mark's face grew red and angry. "In the first departmental meeting he asked me a question about our back-up procedures. I was in the process of telling him when he interrupted me and told me our procedures were ridiculous and I was a dinosaur. In front of the entire goddam department." Mark's hands were gripping the sides of his pants and he was blinking hard. "I'll never forgive him for that." Shaking his head, Mark added, "That's when I had the first fantasy of killing him."

"Go on," I said.

"He's the most despicable person I've ever met," Mark continued. "He has no focus on anything but himself. He has no scruples when it comes to dealing with other people. It's not just me...everyone says so. Going to work every day with him there is a nightmare...you probably want to know why I haven't gotten out of there? Believe me, I tried. I sent out fifty resumes. Believe me, there isn't anything out there for a middle-aged guy who left the technical side of things years ago and is just a manager."

Mark went on to say that "golden handcuffs" were one part of what kept him on his job. His salary was much higher than he could expect to earn anywhere else in the area even if he did find another job. Part of his compensation was paid out in yearly bonuses of company stock that he could only collect, years ahead, with the status as an active employee. His four children were spaced eight years apart, so that Mark could count on paying at least one college tuition for twelve consecutive years. Getting medical coverage at another company for all of his continuing conditions was still another cause for concern.

"Aside from that s.o.b., I really do like my job," Mark continued. "I like the work and I like the people...My crew, they produce, that's why he can't fire me." A sad look came over Mark's face. "I've been here for all these years and I wanted to retire from this job. But I don't know if I'll make it." Tears began to roll down his face. "Believe me, if it goes on like this I'm afraid I'll have a heart attack...or maybe he will fire me and put me out of my misery." Mark's face was screwed up into a tight ball. "But with the kids and all...I'm just not in a position to quit."

For a number of sessions that followed, Mark brought his complaints about Hal. The humiliation seemed to be a sort of hobby with Hal. He was getting off on it, Mark said. The violent fantasies inevitably followed each one of these incidents.

"Have you had any thoughts of how to make things go better with Hal?" I asked.

Mark was vehement. "I don't want to have anything to do with him."

"It's now very important that you get past that attitude," I said.

"What do you mean...why now?" Mark was taken aback.

"You've said more than once that you haven't got a choice about leaving. So you're going to be dealing with Hal under any circumstances. It's time to try to make the best of it."

"But there isn't anything to be done with someone like that," Mark insisted. "He's just pure evil."

"You may be right about Hal. But without question you are wrong about yourself."

"What do you mean?"

"You said `there isn't anything to be done' with him. That is where you are underestimating your own capacity to have an impact. Grossly underestimating."

Mark hesitated. "I guess I have to agree with you as an intellectual proposition," he said. "But I just don't grok it."

Here Mark was using a term coined by the science fiction writer Robert Heinlein in his famous novel "Stranger In A Strange Land." In the book a human being raised on Mars is abruptly transported back to earth and encounters his fellow human creatures and their customs for the first time. Although this stranger can speak human language, he has difficulty grasping ("grokking") the ways of earthlings. The term implies that it is not enough to understand something at the cognitive level; true understanding has an experiential dimension that must be fully lived before real comprehension can be achieved.

"To `grok' something means to know it from the inside," I said. "This all suggests that you need to know the problem with Hal from the inside."

Mark smiled sheepishly. "I have no idea what that means."

"It means that when we meet a serious and seemingly insoluble problem outside ourselves, it's always a good idea to ask if the problem can be overcome by meeting it in ourselves. In this case that would mean looking into yourself to see if you have glossed over the ways in which you can influence the situation favorably, even if you can't change Hal as a person."

"How could I look into that?"

"You could take a situation with Hal that came up, or that you anticipate coming up, and examine it to see where you might have the opportunity to step in and redirect things."

"Oh, sort of like jujitsu, right?" Mark was referring to the Japanese martial art in which the goal is to use an opponent's own weight and strength against himself.

"Yes," I said, "like the part of jujitsu where one learns the technique…by taking an active role in preparation."

It was clear that Mark was coming to the realization that he was not in a situation that could be resolved by brute force, or by a resolute and decisive break. What was not clear to him was that the solution to the conflict would have to come from going into it more deeply, penetrating into it with the utmost clarity and understanding, and then changing it from the inside. He needed to be ready to meet the solution with a creative response, instead of prolonging the conflict by continuing it and carrying it out to a bitter end.

His task was to learn how to influence someone who is intractable and unbending. The secret lay in the method of allowing himself to be influenced first, to allow Hal's essential nature to impress itself upon him, instead of keeping Hal as far as away as possible because of his distasteful unpleasantness. By allowing Hal's very existence to have an effect on him, without conditions or restraints, Mark would learn how to establish contact with Hal, how to understand him and eventually how to influence him in ways that would resolve the conflict in Mark's favor. There was much work to be done before the positive aspects of Mark's contribution at work, and his value as a person, could begin to start influencing Hal. All of this process would mean a development in Mark, in which his contact with his own inner dimensions would be greatly expanded.

"Let's say there is an alternative universe, where I'm not crazed by Hal being my boss? Can we talk about that?" Mark asked in a session not long after. He was ready to explore a way to relate to Hal that might be new and different, more effective.

"Sure," I said. "We have to assume that there is a door through which Hal can be reached. What can it be?"

Mark was smiling. "Do you remember Spock's Vulcan mind-meld on Star Trek?"

"Yes, I do."

On the TV series, Spock would lay his hands on a mute creature from another galaxy and meld his own mind into the being of the creature, for the purpose of establishing communication where none was possible before.

"I think what you're suggesting is that I'm going to have to do a mind-meld with Hal, right?" Mark smiled again. "I guess I've tried wackier things. How would you put it again?"

"You're trying to find the door through which Hal can be reached. The access code. What motivates Hal at the most basic level?"

"He's a pig," Mark said. "...I guess pigs have an appetite."

"What does Hal have an appetite for?"

"He has an appetite for people sucking up to him and doing what he wants." Mark rolled his eyes.

"I would say Hal has a very large unsatisfied appetite, a craving really, for recognition."

"Recognition?"

"Yes, it's what seems to motivate everything about him. He doesn't seem to feel anyone can recognize him adequately for who he is...that makes him angry...and therefore difficult to deal with."

"I don't get it," Mark said.

"The implication here is that you can have what you want from Hal, it might even be appropriate to say you can resolve the problem in totality, if you are willing to give Hal the kind of recognition he craves."

"It can't be that easy," Mark said.

"Who said it was easy?"

During the next period of time at work, Mark discovered what was not easy. He felt the most intense resistances to the idea of being able to change the nature of his own experience of Hal. For now, more than Hal himself, these angry and at times violent rages against the possibility of change, against moving away from the rage, were the new obstacle.

"I feel like it's un-American to try to resolve a problem this way," Mark said. "I can't see John Wayne or Charlton Heston resolving a problem this way."

"Those are very predominant American models of how to behave in a conflict, but fortunately they aren't the only ones."

"What's another example?" Mark asked.

"The framers of the Constitution fought a war for their freedom, but they were still able to recognize that a mechanism was needed to resolve conflicts without resort to war. So as a result we have the `American' way of governing by compromise and checks and balances."

"I suppose," said Mark with a sigh. "I just don't feel like it's manly, to try to snooker somebody into doing something I want."

"You'd rather get the feeling of being manly by smashing him on the head."

Mark shook his head ruefully. "I see what you're getting at, but I still don't know about this..."

During this time, Mark began to have a recurring dream, a dream from which he often woke up to find that his bed sheets were soaking wet. In the dream he was given an assignment at work, and he proceeded to carry it out. The shocking assignment was to choke Hal to death. Several times he woke himself up from the dream at the last moment because he was so horribly disturbed by the terrified look in Hal's eyes, and by the knowledge that he was a murderer once again.

After complaining that the problems with Hal had even followed him into his sleep, Mark asked "What do you think the dream means?"

"I think it means you are trying to `kill' Hal. It's how you are trying to deal with your current life assignment. You're trying to deprive the oxygen from what he represents, choke it off."

"What do you mean?"

"We've talked many times about what Hal represents. A quality of powerful and immovable stubbornness, being incommunicado with the environment, unresponsive. Craving recognition but doing everything to make sure he doesn't get it. You're far from being like Hal overall, but nevertheless there is a quality in you that is very much like him."

"What quality is that?"

"You've been largely unresponsive to your situation. You haven't had the resolve to adapt to it. That's the `Hal' quality that you've been trying to throttle because it's caused you so much pain."

"So you're saying I have a `Hal' in me?"

"Most definitely. Of course, it isn't me saying it. After all, it's your dream."

Mark was silent and thoughtful for a long time.

At last he spoke. "You mentioned `adapting.' I'm not sure I know what that means."

"We know that adapting is the great rule of nature. Creatures that adapt are the ones that survive. The cockroach is the most amazing example--it will feed on practically anything, even the glue on wallpaper. Therefore it has survived for millions of years, long past other species that couldn't adapt to changing conditions."

"How does that apply to me...and to Hal?"

"You haven't adapted, or perhaps we should say the `Hal' in you hasn't. He hasn't permitted you to adapt to the situation and the conditions you are in."

"What you're saying is only common sense...why does it seem like...I can't do it?" Mark was shaking his head. "I guess the first thing..." Mark hesitated for a long moment "...would be to do a mind meld with this part of myself?"

"That sounds right. When you're familiar with the `Hal' qualities in yourself, you will have all the resources you need to deal with the outer Hal."

The session was drawing to a close. Mark rambled on about Hal for a few more moments and then paused. "What's not easy," he said, his voice shaking with emotion, "is to put aside the anger…to get what I want."

After voicing this thought, a look of resolution came over Mark's face. "Ok, I've come this far, I might as well go all the way."

Before the next session Mark cleared his Sunday afternoon calendar of responsibilities with his wife and children and took a long walk in the woods by himself. While he was walking and mulling over his problems with Hal, he noticed a sign in the Forest Preserve marked "Old Lenape Indian Trail." He turned down the direction of this worn path that was lined with brush and birch, oak and ash and maples. He found himself captivated by thoughts of the Indians who must have used this trail, centuries before. Then his thoughts leapt to an old movie he had watched in the middle of the night some weeks before, after waking up from the usual nightmare about murdering Hal.

In the movie there was a scene in which some English colonists were meeting with an Indian tribe in order to trade for furs. Before the furs could be traded there were some elaborate ceremonies. It had occurred to Mark, while he was watching, that no popular film in today's fast paced cinema would devote such lavish attention to the ceremonial details.

The ceremonies took place in a large lodge. There were perhaps forty men, Indians and Englishmen, gathered in a loose circle. First the peace pipe was filled, then lit, and then passed around. Then an Englishman made a flowery speech about the power and grandeur of the realm of the Indian chief; he cited a number of the chief's notable feats of battle as well. Then the Englishman produced a number of gifts from a large trunk.

After many of the gifts had been passed around, there was a stir. Saving the best for last, the Englishman came to the foremost of the gifts. The piece de resistance was a series of small boxes, in which there was an assortment of brightly colored beads. The display of these beads produced grunts of interest and approval from the Indians.

At the conclusion of the ceremonies, which included much ritual and great amounts of food, the trade talk about the price and number of furs was concluded satisfactorily.

As he walked down the old Indian trail, Mark recalled the contempt for the Indians that the English were barely able to contain; they made disparaging comments to one another when they thought the Indians weren't listening.

As Mark returned home, he knew that these scenes from the movie presented more than half the way to a solution to the problems with Hal.

In his next session Mark told me what went on during his afternoon hike in the woods. He noted with a sheepish smile that he couldn't help feeling that this somewhat "cheesy" and stereotypical film nevertheless had an important message for him. He said there was a resemblance between Hal and the Indian chief. They both seemed powerful, immovable, and self-centered.

"Yet the English got what they wanted from him," I noted.

"That's true," said Mark. "Although they had to smoke the peace pipe, and bring gifts."

"And not just any gifts," I said. "They brought gifts that were meaningful to the Indians on their own terms...portraits of the King or the Queen wouldn't have worked."

"I see what you mean," said Mark. "But I don't have something to offer...in the movie they already knew they had to smoke the peace pipe and bring the beads."

"You've had nothing to offer but your contempt."

"I'm afraid you're right there," Mark said. "So what is next?"

"You'll have to experiment, create a new program," I said.

31

Mark's experiment in approaching Hal "through a different door" began on a Wednesday. Mark began the day by "dropping in" on Hal at 7:45 in the morning before anyone else had arrived.

"Had your coffee yet?" Mark asked, holding out up a cup of coffee in each hand. Mark knew perfectly well that Hal got his coffee at precisely eight o'clock every morning.

Hal looked surprised. "Not yet," he said.

Mark sat down in the chair in front of Hal's desk.

"I thought I'd get your advice on the new project," Mark said. "It's going well but there are some things I need your help on." Mark began to outline a number of options that he presented to Hal, who had a strong and certain opinion on each one. The discussion lasted thirty minutes, by which time the coffee was finished and others were arriving in the office to begin the day.

Even though Hal had opted for several decisions that Mark considered "wrong-headed," nevertheless Mark concluded the discussion with a veiled remark: "You've given me a lot to think about...that will be really helpful. Thanks, Hal."

To Mark's astonishment, as he rose to go, Hal said pleasantly "You're welcome, Mark. And remember, I like when you keep me up to date."

There were no embarrassing incidents to report in our next session. Mark recounted the episode with the coffee "gift" and told of his determination to "drop in with some recognition" on a regular basis.

"I feel good about this experiment," Mark concluded. "But I just kind of fell into it. With Hal you never know, he's so unpredictable. He might go back to being an ogre. I need to know more about what goes into an experiment like this--what makes it successful. I need something more than a one-shot deal. I need something more reliable."

During the week, Mark's young son came home with a description of a simple experiment performed in the lower school science lab. From this simple experiment Mark would discover a most profound operational principle of how things on the inside can change things on the outside.

According to Mark's son, the teacher gave the students a sheet of paper, two magnets and some iron filings in a small glass vial. The filings were clumped together like a mound of gray-black pepper. The class poured the iron filings onto the middle of the page, and then placed the magnets under the middle of the sheet of paper.

Now the experiment began. The magnets were moved underneath the paper. There was a bustle of movement. The iron filings in the middle of the page immediately moved themselves into two separate clumps.

Next the magnets were returned to the middle of the page. Once again there was a bustle of movement. The iron filings rearranged themselves into a heap again in the middle of the page, all together in one mound once more.

The students were able to observe that an invisible force, magnetism, could actually rearrange physical matter before their eyes. They learned that the magnets create a force field, a region of space through which a force is operating.

As the teacher explained to his son's class, the force field generated by the magnets was limited to a specific region. The field didn't extend everywhere, but within a specific region the magnets created powerful forces that could rearrange the order and pattern of the physical universe.

In his next session, Mark recounted the story of his son's experiment.

"I'm really onto something here, aren't I?" he asked. "But I'm not sure what it is."

"I think this is addressing that issue of `adaptation' we've been talking about," I said.

"What do you mean?"

"A creative person recognizes that he or she enters into `force fields' all the time in life, and the smart thing to do is to make use of them. We all start out with the all-powerful family dynamics of childhood and then there's the force field of school, with all its regulations and rules and systems, and then there are peers, and later there is the force field of work, where all kinds of forces are at play like the bureaucracy, the system of existing job titles and functions, and so on. Other people, with their attitudes and preferences, are part of the larger external force field into which we enter. Our culture and society at large represent powerful forces exerting a push and pull on us. Even something as simple as the expectation of waiting on a line, or filling out a form is a force field acting on us."

"So it's smart to adapt," said Mark.

"Yes, but that is a word which doesn't really describe what is possible. A really creative person recognizes that by aligning with these force fields, there's much to be gained. The force fields can be manipulated…to give us what we want. That's a whole lot more than what the word 'adapting' seems to imply."

Mark nodded.

"Problems arise when people over-learn the external facts about force fields," I said. "We can become so attuned to the nature of force fields on the outside that we omit the fact that we ourselves are force fields. Physics teaches that each of us, each human being, carries our own electromagnetic charge, and so we alter any force field into which we enter."

"You're on a roll," Mark said. "Go on."

I smiled. It was usually me who said "Go on."

"When we enter into a force field, we change it. We certainly have to learn to recognize the force fields around us. But we also need to realize that we can enter into the world and change it, and we can enter into the world in ourselves, into our own inner being, and our own relationship to our impulses, and rearrange the force field of our own self."

"What about Hal?" asked Mark. "To give him his due, he seems to have a way of relating to force fields too."

"Yes. Some people have largely negative experiences of force fields--

punitive or destructive or just woefully inadequate. Those are the Hals, and they form the expectation that the force fields of the world are only going to deny them what they need or want, or not provide them with their needs, and so they resort to misusing their own force. They have a distorted force field. There is all the difference in the world between simply using force, and working creatively within a force field."

"What would you say is the thing that creates the force...or the force field?" asked Mark.

"Our attitudes. With our attitudes we create the force field through which we experience all the things of our lives, for better or for worse. We find forces in the world and in ourselves that we would do better to rearrange to suit our needs. But if we aren't awake to our capacity to change these things, we fail to make use of our own dynamism."

For many sessions afterwards Mark was engaged in the process of "operationalizing" and "decoding" his powerful discoveries about the nature of force and creative adaptation. He was discovering how to balance the two. During this period the improvements in his relationship with Hal became notably consistent, as did the improvements in his mood and outlook. The fantasies were far fewer.

One of Hal's suggestions, arising from the early morning coffee chats, had worked out well. It was a programming solution that Mark would have implemented on his own, but nevertheless he decided to give the credit to Hal as part of the "peace pipe" experiment.

Mark entered Hal's office at the end of the day with a small bottle of whisky and two plastic cups. "Let's drink a toast to the new project," he said. "Hal, without your suggestions this project might have been a flop. Your contribution was indispensable. Here's to you." These statements were true, because Mark had made sure to draw explicitly on Hal's expertise in the project. Mark poured the whisky and as he handed over a cup, he looked at Hal for a never-to-be-forgotten moment. Hal's face had melted and instead of the "evil" and "sarcastic" mask, Mark saw something he found sad and disturbing. Hal was pathetically grateful for the compliment, but afraid to let his guard down and let go of his pride. His crumpled face seemed weak and inarticulate.

"The guy I saw wasn't threatening at all, just a miserable desperate fool," Mark said in his next session. "I've feel like I've been watching the giant screen of the Wizard, instead of seeing the little man in the booth."

Mark was referring to the famous scene in the Wizard of Oz where Dorothy and her friends discover the Wizard of Oz is a fraud. Here was Mark's much-needed discovery of how much Hal's fearsome qualities resulted from an image that came from within Mark himself.

"It's over," Mark said. "I'll never be intimidated by him again," he said. He talked for this session and the next one about the revolutionary experience of turning the situation with Hal to his own benefit.

"I read somewhere a long time ago that, in the end, all rage is rage against oneself," Mark said. "I kind of feel like that could be true, but I don't 'grok' it."

"Let's introduce a differentiation between justified anger and ongoing rage, rage that takes possession and won't let go," I said. "What could you be enraged at in yourself?"

"I'm very enraged at myself for having been in this position," Mark said. "It's like I can't forgive myself for having been humiliated."

"That's often how we work, as human beings, isn't it? Angry at ourselves for things beyond our control. It isn't 'logical' as Spock would say, but our emotions follow a different kind of logic, a logic of feelings."

"What does that logic say about overcoming rage against oneself?"

"Compassion…embracing ourselves with understanding, empathy, humor, caring…tenderness. All directed to acceptance of our very personal journey and our humanity."

Several sessions later Mark wanted to know "How did it all happen? How did I get past my Hal madness?" he asked.

"It was very powerful that you set yourself up as more than Hal's equal when you offered him the compliment. You reversed the polarities of the force field. When you offered him the compliment, it was as if you were the boss, and he was the employee."

"You're right. I did."

"This might sound crass but the fact is, when you give Hal this kind of recognition, you can get most of whatever you want from him."

"It's not as awful as I thought it would be...being his `boss' I mean." Previously, Mark had been embarrassed by the loss of autonomy in his relationship with Hal. With these new actions, he had claimed his own authority. What was most amazing to Mark was how easily Hal relinquished his tight hold on the reins at work, once Mark was consistently giving Hal the recognition he craved. Hal was now relying on Mark's judgment for more and more of the work in the department, provided that Mark "kept him in the loop."

"I've grokked that I'm a force field," Mark said with pride.

One Friday during this period, Mark's staff and co-workers put on a "surprise" 50th birthday party for him at a local restaurant. Mark could tell the surprise was coming from the way his staff was suddenly at a loss for words when he passed by at work in the days before his birthday.

At the party, Hal was master of ceremonies. Everyone in attendance, including Hal, wore red socks in Mark's honor. Mark was given a seat in the front while the others did a "roast." When it was Hal's turn, instead of the anticipated sarcasm, Hal laid his hand on Mark's shoulders and made an emotional speech about how much Mark had contributed to the company. "I've always told everybody you were the best," Hal said.

Mark couldn't help noting to himself that this was yet one more untruth from Hal's lips. But the meaning of the event was clear to him: he had entered into a situation and had changed it from the inside. Mark's experience of himself as a force field was now a supremely meaningful event, and a supremely meaningful process. It had brought results.

At the end of the period of the discussion about force fields, Mark had another experience of initiating a deeply desired change: the improvement in his physical condition was, in his words, "thrilling and humbling." The night sweats disappeared, the ulcer cleared up, and even his blood pressure lowered to a point where he could go off the medication. He began to be interested in healthy food, started to work out again, and lost a good measure of the weight he had gained since Hal became his boss.

At last Mark was finally able to "grok" that he had learned to be able to withstand the force of his own negative emotions. Mark could now take care of the "inner" business of the soul as well as the "outer" business of the workplace. He could "grok" the exciting experience of overcoming obstacles in himself, leaving him free to explore the ways in which he could create new and unprecedented experiences for himself. Working with the "inner" Hal would be an on-going source of challenges, even though the "outer" Hal was no longer a problem.

One year later Hal was promoted to a new position in another state. According to Mark, many of the others in his department were emailing each other the song "Ding-dong the wicked witch is dead."

"He hasn't changed at all really," Mark said. "He's just found new targets for his sadistic games."

"Yes, all you could do, in this set of circumstances, was to play the game to your advantage. That you did and quite well."

Along with a burst of relief, Mark felt a curious sense of loss when he heard the news of Hal's departure. Mark realized what Hal's value had been to him. From the point of view of self-mastery, Hal had been heaven-sent because he was the occasion for so much development on Mark's part, so much expansion of his realm of understanding and action, of his own capacity for creating a new way of living with greater freedom. Mark had grown both attached to and respectful of this problem he had conquered. "Compassion…without blindness to the 'bad' Hal," was how he put it. He was now able to see Hal as a person with a soul, however distorted.

Mark was called on to speak at Hal's going away party. During his toast, Mark told the assembled guests:

"I can truly say I've learned more from working with Hal than any of my previous bosses. Hal, you've been a catalyst for my growth in ways I wouldn't have believed possible. Believe me, I appreciate you more than you can know." While Hal grew tearful, Mark held up the fingers of his hand spread apart in Spock's Vulcan symbol for peace, and concluded his toast "Hal, live long and prosper."

Perhaps the best sign for a good prognosis for Mark had been the state of his conscience about the violent fantasies. If he had been content to just "enjoy" the fantasies at the level of revenge, it was likely that he would have never been able to undertake the challenging process of change that he underwent. In actuality his conscience had bothered him a great deal. He knew not only that something was wrong, but that something must be done to correct it. That was an indication of a conscience in good working order, of a relationship to the inner world that acted as a guide and a motivator. Mark knew he was capable of more, more than living a life of angry fantasies. Even trapped in his most extreme emotions about Hal, even in the "blast furnace" of his own emotions, there was still a part of his view of himself as a positive person that held his allegiance. As he said, he was determined to hold on to the experience of himself as a decent person.

The episode with Hal led to a new channel for the energy that had gone into the negative fantasies. The rechanneling of this energy amounted to a new premise about what can be done about things that are seemingly set in stone. All this resulted in a new birth of hope as a living daily experience for Mark as well as a new sense of competency. The events with Hal were a catalyst for a change within Mark that was permanent and enduring. He had "mind-melded" with his own capacity to be a force field within himself, and in the world.

Near the end of our work together, Mark spent a few sessions looking back with a new clarity at his journey in life.

"I've grokked a new perspective on what my life has been about," he said. "I can sum it up in a single sentence."

"What's that?"

"Rage is a creative act that is blocked."

I was in awe, in awe of what can happen in the human psyche, under the right conditions. This sentence summed up his learning, and his path forward. I looked up at the fireworks and thought that Matisse too might have been enraged with his limitations, had he not found a way to express himself with his cut-outs.

In his last session Mark said:

"As a creative person, now I feel like I want to do everything I really need to. Is that a bizarre thing for a 51-year-old man to say?" He paused. "I know, I know, you'll ask me, what do you think?"

"What do you think?" I asked.

"This is realistic…I'm not talking about anything extra-galactic…this is very realistic. Believe me, there really is a force inside."

-Chapter Three-
"What Do You Do When Life Craps Out On You?"

How and why does life demand that we renew ourselves? What happens when we resist a profound inner demand to move on, to change, to experience a new way of living? This is the story of a man who learned there is more than one satisfying way to make new things real.

Philip King was a legend in the toy industry. It all began in his mid-thirties while he was working for a toy and notions manufacturer. He and his wife took a week's vacation in a small town in the Irish countryside. While walking along a dark country road in County Donegal, Philip saw a house with a light on and, being the curious sort, he walked up to a window and peered in. In the corner of a room he saw women sewing and talking. He was spotted, and he and his wife were waved in. Philip was delighted to discover that the Irish women were making extraordinarily beautiful dolls for their children by hand, according to the old traditions.

He returned to the U.S. with samples and a tremendous enthusiasm for the Irish dolls. With the approval of his company, Philip put the town and its neighbors to work around the clock producing a line of hand-made dolls with beautifully tailored clothing.

The first shipments were snapped up in both the United States and Europe, and the resulting publicity sensation ensured a lasting success. Philip single-handedly created a new marketing niche where none existed before: children, adults and collectors all vied for the limited number of the very special dolls. Soon Philip opened an Asian factory to produce inexpensive replicas for the mass market.

As a result of the spectacular increase in sales, Philip leapfrogged over others in the company and was named president and chief executive officer while still in his early forties.

With his distinguished silver-gray hair, patrician charm, and good breeding, Philip was much in demand on local community boards and business associations in northern New Jersey where he raised his children. He was a person whose enthusiasm was captivating, and highly effectual. He built a twelve-room Georgian-style house of his own design in Northern New Jersey with two tennis courts, covered in winter with "bubbles" to allow for cold weather play and for the huge cocktail parties he threw on a regular basis.

As Philip would recall later, it was a heady time. Whenever he returned to Ireland, the people in the villages turned out as if the Pope had arrived. At the company, dolls were being shipped by the truckload. Each new related product, especially the doll's accessories, was a smash hit. Foreign competitors had not yet entered the upscale American market and Philip was able to dominate the market by himself. He was lionized in the business press as the embodiment of the new breed of dynamic young CEOs.

Within a few years Philip decided to expand into other areas: he began to preach the gospel of diversity to his product and marketing people. Soon the company was competing with much larger and more well-established toy makers in high-volume, low-margin product areas. Philip's energies were consumed with items such as plastic warriors and small board games, and faddish point of sale items such as extra-sour gum and superhard bouncing balls. Philip tried with only the most limited success to compete with the giant firms in producing these items. His costs were high and his margins were low. But the problems hardly seemed to matter as the dolls marched into the stores and were snapped up.

During this time Philip's four children grew to maturity and his marriage began to fall apart. He carried on a long affair with a secretary who was twenty years his junior. At last, he divorced and married his secretary, a woman he genuinely loved. His first wife took the divorce very hard. She started drinking heavily and would often call him late at night with a string of venomous accusations. "She turned into a witch," he told his many sympathetic friends. Finally he got an unlisted number.

Meanwhile it had taken the other toy companies nearly a decade but at last they caught up with Philip at the high end of the market. Consumer loyalty to his brand began to fade. Knock-offs of his exquisite dolls appeared at discounted prices. Philip's dolls were supposed to be one-of-a-kind but now lookalikes could be easily obtained through major toy distributors. Clothing separates offered by competitors began to outsell the matching sets sold by Philip's line. Then Philip and his company took a double whammy.

First electronic toys started to capture an ever larger share of the market. Philip himself had no feel for electronic games and simply ignored them. At the same time a prolonged recession began to dampen consumer demand for toys. Philip and the company were unprepared for both. In three years his company went from record profitability to massive losses.

The final blow came when the chairman of Philip's company organized a buyout by a large European concern. After the first meeting with the new European chairman, who was entirely taken with electronic toys, Philip knew he was out. He agreed to a severance package that was "more than fair."

It was a painful departure but within three weeks Philip's legendary status as an incomparable marketer produced a new offer from a huge competitor who was also bleeding red ink.

"After six months (at the new company), I feel like I've been here all my life," Philip said with enthusiasm.

The losses were mounting at the new company, but Philip was still in the honeymoon period, so no one could hold him accountable. Younger executives marveled at the serene way he presided over meetings. There seemed to be no problem that he had not encountered before, no problem that could not be overcome effortlessly.

Having grasped the lay of the land at the new company, Philip decided the company needed to pin its hopes on an area that for them was uncharted territory despite their many corporate divisions. The new venture he recommended was a massive foray into...expensive, handmade dolls. With his charm, enthusiasm and unquestioned expertise, Philip was easily able to win over the chairman and the board of directors.

He committed a major portion of the company's resources into dolls made by workers in overseas plants in the Far East. The results were swift and catastrophic. Despite a costly advertising and marketing campaign the company failed to gain market share, the dolls piled up in warehouses, and the debt he had incurred was triple the level of his predecessor. When the parent company decided the investments could not be recovered, Philip was out again in just two years.

In order to save face, the company created a special division just for him: Philip King Toys. With a staff of three, Philip would have the opportunity to develop new products on a very limited budget. The company still believed in his "creative vision" of the toy market, even though they had no faith in him as a corporate manager.

Once on the new job his second wife noticed a change in him. He was no longer his ebullient self, rising every morning with an eagerness to get to work, ready to tackle a long day of meetings and projects, and then just as eager after work to play tennis or plan a next cocktail party. When his enthusiasm had been nearly depleted, she arranged for him to see a physician. The physician offered to write a prescription for a popular anti-depressant. Philip declined angrily. Then Philip's wife cajoled him into calling me for a first appointment. As he said himself, he would never have gone if it were up to him.

In the first session, Philip summarized his problems:

"If only I could find another doll. I need to find the equivalent of a new doll and a new Ireland somewhere." That was Philip's description of his problem. He gave a summary of his career and finished by putting his head in his hands. "So that's it," he concluded, "that's where I am. I need something to get me back in the game, back where I can manage a company."

It would hardly be an exaggeration to say that Philip's old success possessed him. His mind and his soul had been "bewitched" by what had happened previously. The obsession showed itself in every facet of his life. His monomania around his Ireland success had led to him to a state where all things revolved around finding another place like it. Everyone he met at cocktail parties was "mined" for information. Every person, every book, every article and news program carried a potential for revealing where the next success might be, and Philip's thoughts traveled around this one subject like captive planets around a dying sun. The equilibrium of his life had been disturbed and he had no means for restoring it.

It seemed that when Philip peered into that room in the Irish countryside, he saw more than women sewing dolls and more than an unusual business opportunity. Philip saw the possibility of how in life something insubstantial, a mere "image" or "idea," can be turned into a tangible reality. Like many another enterprising person, and like many an entrepreneur, he was emotionally gripped by this experience. It brought him an excitement that held a greater appeal than money or status, an appeal greater even than the pleasures that companionship with other people might bring him.

As a result of his early success at converting something insubstantial into something practical and substantive, the restlessness and the discontent that had dogged his life were seemingly banished by excitement and enthusiasm. His joy was generated by the process of experiencing himself as the author of this experience. After Ireland it seemed to Philip that at last everything would be "all right." For a long time, it was. Then the joy ebbed and the experience failed him.

In subsequent sessions, I encouraged Philip to branch out in his description of himself, and so he gave an account of his current family life and his college years. After a number of sessions about his family, I noted:

"You haven't said anything about your first wife."

Philip looked surprised. "What does she have to do with it?"

"Let's find out."

"Well, she's turned into a fanatic. She's never going to get over the divorce. She got my unlisted number from the kids and calls me two or three times a week, late at night, bombed out of her skull. She keeps asking what went wrong, what could she have done differently."

"What do you say?"

"I tell her that I haven't any idea. We were too young back then. She should just get on with her life. She's an albatross around my neck. Most of the time I just hang up the phone on her."

"What would you say is at the core of your ex-wife's problem?"

"She just can't get on with it. Let it go, you know? She's trying to breathe life into a corpse."

"Yes, that's a good way to put it. She's obsessed with the past. I wonder if dolls and Ireland aren't the same thing for you."

"What do you mean?"

"I wonder if it's time for you to let the past bury the corpse of this great success you had. Let it go. Let new success be born."

"Never," said Philip. "That's the thing I built my whole career on. I'd be a nobody without it."

"Do you believe your first wife is a nobody without you as her husband?"

"No. Of course not."

"Well?"

"But I can't give this up. I owe everything to it...You can't seriously mean it?"

For weeks, Philip was distraught. In each session he argued that the source of his success could not be abandoned, that he would be without hope, without a future. The old formula was best, he said. There weren't any new formulas out there, he insisted. In one session, he declared: "There aren't any second acts in American life."

At last he stopped coming for his weekly session: he took flight. First it was a doll-hunting trip to Europe. Then he went to Asia. But on his return his feelings of dismay worsened. After more than a year he returned, and this time he called the decision his own. He was dispirited but noticeably calmer.

Philip reported that a thought had occurred to him while visiting the Indonesian island of Bali. He had stopped in Denpasar, the capital, to see if the Balinese, famed for their extraordinary dancing, music and crafts in honor of their deities, were a possible source for new toys. On a trip to the countryside, a Balinese dealer told him that the joy of dancing, carving and painting in honor of the gods was the driving force behind the happiness that Philip noted on the faces of the Balinese artisans.

"I would like something like that," he sighed one day. He seemed about to discuss that happiness but then returned to his old obsession and added, "But there's no market here for what they make."

In the course of his travels Philip had acquired an old green parrot of a kind known as a "lovebird." From one of its previous owners the parrot had learned many of the usual expressions that are taught to talking birds. Among these was "You dummy." The bird also picked up some of Philip's characteristic expressions: "I need another Ireland" was one. Philip said, with a hearty laugh, that during the year away he was reminded of his obsessions when the parrot would intone "I need another Ireland, you dummy."

After chuckling for some time, Philip was quiet and then seemed to "drop down" into a new state of reflection.

"Why has life crapped out on me?" he wanted to know.

"What do you mean?"

"I feel like my fate has deserted me. I was meant to be successful. Now this. I mean I was going along, reasonably happy, and I felt like I was living the life I was supposed to be living. Then everything deserted me."

"Go on."

"What I'm living now feels very strange, like it isn't me. I don't recognize my life anymore. I'm being forced to go forward into a life that seems very strange to me."

"What could account for that?"

Philip ignored the question. "I don't have a company to run anymore. I don't have any of my old direction. I'm not even head of a family anymore. I'm getting older and I don't know what I'm heading toward." He paused. "So why has life crapped out on me?"

There was a long pause.

"It seems that repeating yourself is a fate too low for you," I replied.

"What do you mean?"

"Something more is being asked of you, something more than repeating your old success."

"What is that?"

"It's not clear yet, but it appears that you need to create a new means for the expression of your energy and your enthusiasm."

Philip had been like an ancient nomad who sits by a dry well, waiting for an underground stream to change back to a course abandoned years ago. The source of his enthusiasm and elation was comparable to this subterranean stream. As streams do, this one had veered away. Rather than conduct a vigil at its last manifestation, Philip needed to heed the call to move on, to tap the serpentine underground stream of vitality that is a potential within each of us, where we can find a fresh, bubbling source of life.

But how to do it? He wanted to know.

"What would you say the Ireland experience meant to you?" I asked in a session some weeks later.

"It was the greatest thing in my life, the thing that made my career."

"How would you describe what happened?"

"I guess I was inspired. I saw the possibility of something and then I made it happen."

"A most worthy process."

"Yes." Philip shrugged. "But then I failed to make it happen again."

There was a long pause.

"What inspired you to get into the toy business in the first place?" I asked.

Philip chuckled. "I've often asked myself why would a full-grown man be attracted to toys...actually I saw this as a business where the imagination is all. That's what appealed to me then and still does." His voice became lower. "When I was a child, I loved my toys very much."

"How do toys figure into your life now?"

Philip shrugged. "Only in a professional way."

"Do you recall any of those toys you loved?"

"If I tried I could, maybe, but I don't know."

"Have you tried?"

"Not really."

"Perhaps you should."

After this session, Philip bought a spiral notebook of paper and a set of colored pens and pencils, and began to go back in his memory in order to dredge up the toys and games of his childhood. To help envision his early years, he drew watercolors of himself on the playgrounds of his childhood, and at play in his childhood bedroom where a large green toy shed held all of his treasures.

"Most of these toys don't exist anymore," Philip said, "except at collector's shows. So I had the idea of making one or two."

Philip took up modeling clay and began to spend his evenings recreating the toys of his childhood. The first toy he made was from late childhood. It was a roller-coaster with cars, a toy he admired immensely. Then he began to press back earlier into childhood. He carved several spinning-tops from wood, and painted one bright blue, another bright red, and another green with yellow stripes.

It had been peculiarly satisfying, Philip reported in his next session, to attach the steel heads to the tops and to sand the tops into working order.

When Philip wound one of the tops with string and put it into play, a remarkable process occurred. While the striped top was spinning, he experienced a feeling that was at once familiar and strange. He was transported back to himself as a little boy, standing in front of a spinning top and marveling at it. While the top was spinning he had the very odd sensation of watching himself as a boy, while still experiencing himself as a middle-aged man.

The extraordinary "double" feeling evaporated when the top fell over on its side and stopped. So he spent several hours winding and spinning the top and lost himself in the experience of "unwinding" buried memories, along with sensations and feelings from his childhood around the age of six or seven.

He remembered the names of boyhood friends whom he hadn't thought about in many years. Then a cascade of memories and experiences started appearing before his mind's eye; he had to write as fast he could to make notes on them. The experience was so vivid that he said he could remember a pair of corduroy pants he wore then, and how the wale fabric felt on his legs; he could "see" the contents (compass and pencil, small flat-edged scissors, red pencil sharpener) of a notebook binder he carried to school with a leather exterior casing and a wide brass zipper. This was all from a man who had earlier claimed not to recall anything at all from his childhood years.

In his next session, Philip said in a voice filled with awe:

"Part of me is still back there, standing over my toys. And playing in the schoolyard." He was amazed to discover that these experiences still carried a "wallop."

One memory in particular came to the foreground. Philip remembered an incident, he said it actually might have been repeated more than once, when he lost some of his toys.

It happened in the schoolyard, as Philip came upon some older boys playing with tops. A circle had been drawn with a stick in the dust on the sidewalk. The boys were playing a game in which they threw down their spinning tops and attempted to drive other spinning tops out of the circle. The winners got to keep the tops that they drove out.

Philip wanted to play with the older boys, and so he risked his precious tops and lost. He ran home crying. But he was mocked at home for not taking his loss like a man, and so he received no comfort.

As he told this story to me, Philip said the pain of the loss was like today's pain. Just as he was "still standing there" watching the marvels of his boyhood, the boyhood pain too was alive in him nearly fifty years later.

In his pain he still wanted to reach out and grab his tops from the other boys and run away. He felt torn between the desire to "cheat" by somehow getting back the tops that he loved so much, and the desire to take his loss "like a man," as he had to admit, some of the older boys seemed to do.

For quite some time after this episode, he watched the games of the older boys from afar, filled with many emotions: anger, frustration, longing, an urge for action, a sense of defeat. He watched closely and began to mimic their postures: the hitching up of pants, the blowing on dice or marbles for luck, the cries of "Luck be a lady."

At home he drew a circle in the dust, threw down some marbles, and played out the drama of the game, enacting all the roles and postures.

When at last he was nearly as old as the current group of players, he finally reentered a marbles game and played with a fierce determination. He "took all the marbles," shoving them into an old cigar box, leaving the other boys with nothing left to continue the game for the day. The recall of this memory left Philip choked with emotion.

In the sessions that followed Philip "forgot" for the first time his obsession with finding a way back to managing a large company. His obsession had transferred itself, so to speak, into reviving these old memories and experiences. These were the subject of his concentrated energies, and he pursued them with the same relentlessness.

"What were the consequences of these losses, back then?" I wanted to know. "How did you react?"

"I was very wary," Philip said. He actually narrowed his eyes. "I was suspicious of other kids, and I didn't like them to play with my toys. My parents used to get on me about that."

Philip had been spending his evening hours creating a catalogue of the memories, arranged chronologically, and now he attempted to push them back as far as he could. An earliest memory now came to the fore:

At the age of three or four, Philip awoke very early on a spring day before everyone else in the house. Without waking anyone, he let himself out the backdoor as the dawn was breaking and walked through the dewy grass to the garden. The padded feet of his pajamas were soaking wet by the time he reached the crossing rows and tall stakes of the garden. As the sun rose, songbirds were twittering in the elms, willows, and oaks near the house. In the vegetable patch a warm and fragrant breeze moved through the leafy plants. Philip saw that "bunnies" were quietly feeding on the lettuce and carrot tops. The rays of the sun crept closer to the garden as Philip squatted on his knees, and he was filled with a tremendous but quiet excitement. He watched these wondrous creatures, who didn't pay him any attention at all, until the sun became strong and the "bunnies" hopped away.

Philip went into the house for breakfast and told everyone (his mother and father, the cook, the handyman) about the "bunnies." That was the end of the memory, but traveling back into the experience now as an adult, he became aware that he was frustrated because there was something he couldn't convey to the adults, something in the experience that he couldn't get them to share.

Here was another moment when time seemed to stand still. In the German language, such moments are called the "Sternstunde," the star hours, the moments when the time quality of the stars seems to come down to earth.

The recollection of these memories had a profound effect on Philip. His obsession with the externals of life, with success, was "relativized" by these engrossing memories. His experience of obsession was now a step closer to its underground source within.

In subsequent sessions it became clear that the loss of his toys helped to solidify Philip's already well-formed life premise. Life has ruthlessness and uncertainty and loss in it, he had discovered. While these experiences had pained him and frightened him, they had also helped to make him wary and determined. As a result he worked at cultivating his most natural talent, his charm, to get what he wanted. A procession of fearful experiences had followed in Philip's boyhood, including the loss of his father's business and his childhood home, followed by a traumatic "banishment" to a boys' boarding school, and these experiences had only reinforced his "dog-eat-dog" philosophy.

At the same time, much of his experience of joy had also gone underground. The hauntingly beautiful moments when he shared in the beauty of the world, when he knew of life in harmony, had been driven "below" by the traumatic events that followed. But the influence of the moment of the "bunnies" had not disappeared; it had formed part of Philip's underlying life premise. The early experiences of joy gave the subterranean impetus to his obsessive search for what could make him happy. With the serendipitous Ireland experience there appeared to be a moment when joy could finally make its return, when the world of harmony, of nature and of "all the marbles" could be his. This was what Philip had been seeking since early childhood: the return to an elemental experience of life. As he said "There is a snake in every paradise. I wanted to drive out mine, like St. Patrick in Ireland."

The Dawn of a New Life

Again and again in his sessions Philip now returned to the earliest memories. He described his recollection of his very early childhood as "saturated with joy." Much of what a young child experiences had become accessible to him; for example, he described the overall pleasure in the body-tone of himself as a young child as he romped through a day of playful activities. He was now obsessed with the desire to pull this experience into the present, across the great divide that separates the child from the man.

"The idea of returning to this joy seems to have caused a problem," I said.

"What do you mean?" said Philip with his characteristic suspicious air.

"You can't literally re-experience those things again...and thank goodness you can't. You'd have to regress totally back to the state of a child. Your task is to encompass this desire at a different level."

"What level is that?"

"The level of spontaneous living in the present. When you experience joy today, you are just as much creating something new as returning to something from before," I continued. "Sure, there is something in common among all experiences of joy, or pain for that matter. They all come from the `mother lode' so to speak. But to do it justice, the joy you experience today is not just a joy because it enables you to return and re-experience what you felt as a boy. It's something you generate now, something of yourself you pour into life today."

"I suppose that's what makes the Balinese so happy."

"Presumably. We can be sure the things they do wouldn't keep on making them happy if they could only long for the joys of the past."

"True..." said Philip.

"The great lesson from childhood for adults is from play...when children play they are creating a new reality...in the same way you did around the Ireland experience. You do have to recreate the Ireland experience...but not literally."

"I wish I knew what that means."

"It means giving yourself occasions for joy...based on your current life."

"But that's very difficult."

"Yes, it's much easier to try to dredge up the glories of the past."

Philip blew out a long gasp of air.

The session was drawing to a close.

"There is a dawn, like the miraculous one you experienced as a child, every new day," I said. "The meaning of that fact is worth a lifetime of contemplation."

"I want so much to be alive the way I was when I was young," Philip said. It was a session some time later. "But in a way that is right for me now."

"Yes."

"You've helped me to become aware that I've been acting as if I had no chance for new possibilities."

"Yes."

"What would a different experience be? It's something I think about now when I spin the tops. What is the source of joy?"

"What have you come up with?"

"Only a feeling of being deprived of something...like there's always something more, just out of reach."

"I would say that everything we experience, even when we experience it fully like your feeling of being alive in every pore when you were young, always points to still more experiences. There is no end...there's always more. The potential experiences in the future expand as we ourselves do."

Philip eyes widened. "I see," he said. Then he added, "That means there's always more...more joy too."

Based on all the hard work, work that often seemed tedious and repetitive, work in which the improvements seemed far from dramatic, an enormous shift had now taken place in the subterranean ground of Philip's obsession. As a result he began to have an experience of relief, of a burden being lifted.

The relief was apparent in a discussion of the ways he had imitated the clothes, the walk, and the attitude of the older boys. He had been highly aware of everyone else's experiences, and the ways in which they were out of his reach. He had indeed registered the fact that there is always more to experience in life, extending infinitely, but he had felt this was a fact only because of something about him, something that was awry within him. He had drawn too personal an explanation for one of the most essential objective facts about human experiencing.

With a burst of relief, Philip said:

"We all experience the world as always unfinished," he said. "It isn't just me." It was now apparent that this too personal explanation had dogged his life. Here was the underlying premise with which he had framed the quality of his own experiencing as faulty and inadequate, as frustrating and limited. He had fought mightily against it in much of his life but after the collapse of his Ireland vision he had at last succumbed.

Once freed from this personal explanation, he was now able to experience himself as a participant in the long historical tradition of mankind, the "always more" that stretches out equally into the past and the future, the very source of joy. Philip was at last embracing the fact that like the dawn, experience is self-renewing, and that he wouldn't run out of new experiences if he let Ireland go. Here was a new premise that was broad and wide enough to encompass life as it is. As he said, he could make this "idea" into a reality and not have it crap out on him. He could tap into it for new experiences of starshine.

During this period Philip's enthusiasm for life came back on a day-to-day basis.

"This job is a gift," he said. "I've finally realized it."

"How so?"

"I've got a chance to do what I really love...create toys that have something special in them...I feel like the universe provides...I have a wonderful place to express that the imagination is all...I didn't really enjoy all that corporate-schmorporate stuff anyway. Oh it's true I like being in charge," he said, smiling, "but only if it's close to the imagination part of it."

In fact Philip's new line of toys was of such high quality and unusual design that they once again attracted the interest of both adults and children, although on a much smaller scale than the Irish dolls. Once again he had the experience of both financial and critical success, and the return of this experience was "much more satisfying than the first time."

During the previous few years Philip had been gradually realizing how much his second wife cared for him, and what a blessing her love had been for him. An episode in which he expressed his own love for her showed how much he had been able to grasp what it is that makes for passion and meaning.

One evening he felt a powerful upsurge of love for his wife, and had a fantasy of taking her for a second time to Bali, so that he might pick for her a fragrant bouquet of tropical flowers. He had a feeling of disappointment and let-down when he realized that for the time being, such a trip was not possible. They were living within a budget for the first time in their marriage. Then his new ability to penetrate to the meaning of the fantasy came to the fore. Taking his wife by the hand, he sat her down in an armchair in their living room.

"Will you try something with me?" he asked her.

"What?" she asked.

"I want you to close your eyes...ok, now see us packing up a full load of suitcases, we're going to Bali...now we're getting on the first leg of the flight...it's all those long hours on the plane...drinking lots of water...playing cards...now we're arriving at last, late at night...we're in the guest house, we crash into bed...now it's the next morning, one of those incredible dawns in Bali...you're just waking up...I've been up earlier...I went out into the back where the flowers grow. I picked up a bouquet of the most exquisite ones just for you...open your eyes, darling, here it is."

Handing her the "bouquet" Philip kissed her.

"Oh, it's the most beautiful gift," said his wife. Philip's wife took the "bouquet" and danced with it around the room.

For the first time in as many years as he could remember, Philip felt relaxed.

Discussion

As an enterprising person, Philip had been gripped all of his adult life by the possibility of fashioning something real, i.e. a business success, from something insubstantial. Far from knowing relaxation, he knew only about this possibility through obsession. He was not connected to the way joy results from turning an image or an idea into something real, not just in business but in life as a whole. His task was to master an approach to the "insubstantial" things of life besides enacting them literally and concretely.

By the time our work together ended, he had experienced the benefits of imagining things further. He could give his wife the meaning itself, and its accompanying joy, without the trip and without the flowers, and so they could both share the passion and meaning, pass them back and forth, and create still more. In this way, the images that come from the soul can enrich us in extraordinary ways.

As Philip said, he was now living on a different plane, a plane on which he could appreciate his own role in creating happiness. Behind Philip's lifelong obsession, perhaps behind every obsession, was an unused power to create this meaning. For Philip, the self-generation of joy and passion had to become a reality and a satisfaction in its own right.

One of the remarkable facts about human life is that the essential energy for a "first" pattern of living can recede, at first in a subterranean way, then increasingly more obviously. If this occurs, then a new challenge presents itself: aligning oneself with a "second" life premise. This entails moving onto a higher level of consciousness with renewed contact with the soul.

The nature of the soul is that its streaming and passionate energy, so alive in children, stays underground in adults even if unlived. This was Philip's great discovery with his revival of childhood experiences and memories. There is a trap door, so to speak, in our most important images that leads deep into our important memories and formative experiences. Philip's "second" task in adulthood was to tap into that stream of passion consciously. The source of joy, and of passion, is at the mysterious core of every human being, eternal and unlimited, waiting to be tapped. There is always more of it, and it never runs out. No human being can exhaust it, nor reach its ultimate source. These facts should not alter our commitment to the fact that we can make a very good attempt at living the joy and passion that are within our own capacities.

As Philip learned, unthinking repetition is the enemy of the soul, but what could be more human than to retry a pattern or formula that has worked well in the past? We might well ask, what kind of person could get caught in repeating a formula long past its usefulness? Only someone who has never grasped the range and extent of their own power to create new patterns. That was Philip's predicament: he was not attuned to the creative movement of life and his own role in it.

Like many people, Philip formed an image of how success is achieved and then without realizing it, he began to worship this image.

This is the danger when a single image seems to promise us everything we want. This "graven" image (the image of his happening upon the Irish doll makers and all that ensued) had an enslaving effect on his otherwise creative and fertile mind. Rather than being one of the people who routinely dismiss images, Philip was enamored of them to the point of idolatry.

His recollection of his childhood toys and experiences restored a unity to his life that had been split apart as so often happens: childhood split apart from adulthood. By the time he was finished, he had restored a sense of the ongoing drama of his life so that all the developments made sense, even the experience of life coming to a halt.

The image of the Balinese served the purpose of introducing a positive image of how human beings can have a lifelong commitment to an adventurous and fulfilling way of living. It gave Philip a new and remarkably vivifying image of life as always "unfinished." This image replaced his illusion that there are no "second acts" in life.

When Philip created the special moment with his wife, he had arrived at the stage of the journey where we generate new images and change the energy flow of the moment in a more suitable direction. His second career was filled with the same creative dynamism. He created a new premise that life is newly created by us, just as each day is newly created. In this way he met the great challenge of his life: to live passionately at play in the game of life with a focus on how life is lived.

-Chapter Four-
Some People Only Get on the Path to the Soul through Tragedy

Prologue: Changing Fate In The "Nick" Of Time

According to the ancient Greeks, a man's or a woman's fate is given as a gift. The gift package or "share" of fate for each person is dispensed by three female beings, who are neither gods nor human, known as the Fates. Their task is to allot the gifts of life from the gods.

The process of getting a fate was compared to the process of preparing cloth. At the very beginning, the gift or allotment of a person's fate is bunched-up in a large mass of raw material like unprocessed wool. This messy clump is the gross portion of a person's fate, its overall weight in coarse strands. The weight of this clump of fate is assigned on the scale of Lachesis, the disposer of lots.

Now a hand-off process begins. Lachesis gives the still unrefined portion of fate to Clotho who spins out the heap of raw thread with her distaff and spindle. She transforms the fate into fine threads.

The share of fate is now ready for Atropos, whose name means the inexorable one, the one who is unmoved by pity. Atropos binds and weaves the threads of fate on a loom. With her shuttle, Atropos weaves the woof about the warp threads, making the pattern which is the tapestry of a person's fate. Woven into the tapestry are such things of fate as character, physical make-up, and environment.

Atropos also weaves the element of Time into the tapestry with the warp threads. In this way the length of a person's life is also woven directly into the fabric of fate.

Originally, the ancients believed that all this happens before life unfolds. In later times, the tasks of the Fates were described as on-going during the actual life of a man. For example, Atropos was described with great horror as cutting the thread of fate without mercy at the end of life.

But in earlier times it was believed that after all the characteristic aspects of fate were assigned at birth, there was just one final step: a person needed to be "bound" to their fate, wrapped up in the fabric of their fate as in a winding sheet.

Being "bound" to one's fate was a necessity because, like woven cloth, a fate could actually be loosened. It was miraculously true that in the overall weave of fate, there was a space between the warp and woof threads known as the "nick." Since the Fates also wove Time into the loom with the warp threads, that meant that in the "nick of Time" there are gaps, or ports, through which non-fated opportunities might be seized or lost by man. These are the moments when a person is not "bound to do it," not bound to do fate's bidding.

With this provision for freedom, a man could make trouble or good for himself beyond that which was fated. With freedom comes the fourth and final portion of fate, the portion where what matters most is a man's or woman's own art at weaving life's tapestry. When a man enhanced or diminished his fate, the ancients said he "clothed" himself in the qualities of his actions; he "wore" his courage or cowardice, pride or humility. And when he died and was buried naked, he was literally wound and wrapped up in a long burial sheet, clothed in nothing but this tapestry of fateful qualities.

Although there was this provision for freedom among the ancients, there was limited interest in how fate and freedom are woven together. There was not even a specific name for the unified tapestry woven through the combining of fate and freedom.

Today we have a new interest in the unitary process of weaving, binding and "wearing" in which a man or woman mixes fate and freedom together. We want to feel that we are maximizing our freedom as much as possible. We too lack a specific name for combining freedom and fate, but when the weave works and includes both, we find ourselves living with deep meaning. Since they were more familiar with how the process doesn't work, how a man or woman fails to introduce meaning into the givens of fate, the Greeks attributed this failure mainly to "hubris" the wrong kind of pride, a pride that leads a man or woman to encroach on the territory of the gods. In such a case, defiance of the gods brings tragedy.

In this story we have the opportunity to see that even tragedy, resulting from hubris, can offer meaning. In fact, some people only get on the path to the soul through tragedy.

John Ionikos grew up in the world of the male. The second oldest of four boys, he attended a famous all-boys prep school, had been a star athlete and had spent much of his youth in organized sports, and had grown up in a profession--the securities business--that was dominated by men. He even had three boys of his own.

John came from a well-connected family. His father was a prominent figure in the securities business, as were several uncles and his grandfather. There were Mayflower descendants on his mother's side. The family dominated their small Connecticut town on school boards, in town government, and in business. There were streets named for John's maternal ancestors.

Very tall, broad-shouldered, and handsome with regular features and a cleft chin, John had more than a bit of a swagger in his walk. At his securities firm he was known as a "hotshot" and with his quick mind, impatient manner, and imposing size, he often intimidated others into agreeing with him. He had several other idiosyncrasies that sat uneasily with his colleagues.

Without warning he would walk out of other people's offices in mid-sentence--theirs or his--and leave without saying a good-bye. It left people unnerved and anxious, uncertain what had actually happened.

He would also break into bouts of cursing with both women and men, in particular reserving his choicest epithets for the "assholes" he disapproved of, and for the bureaucrats who stood in the way of the real "doers."

He would often put his large feet up on the desk, in his own office or in the offices of others, so that his expensive alligator shoes stood between him and the face of a colleague. It was still another of his unsettling idiosyncrasies that caught people off guard.

John was equally unpredictable when it came to warmth. At times he would be preoccupied with his own thoughts and would walk right by people he knew well without so much as a "hello." Sometimes it was a gruff "yeah," when he met people in the hallway.

Then at other times he could be spontaneously charming, throwing his arm around a colleague, and offering genuine appreciation: "that was great work, buddy." In particular, he could be extraordinarily loyal to people who had worked for him. Whenever any of his former employees needed help with finding a new job, John extended himself much more than others by calling his contacts for any leads, and by staying in touch with a brief but unpredictably timed phone call. He was a self-described "big softy" when it came to the troubles of anyone who looked up to him or leaned on him for help.

His career was progressing rapidly and "on track" until one day he uttered one of his gruff "yeahs" to a new secretary, Marlanna, who was an immigrant from another country. Marlanna had not been "enculturated" into the world of the securities business and the world of the male. She took offense at his impoliteness but said nothing. Then the next day he sat down next to her desk and put his feet up on the "In" box on her tidy desk.

"Where the fuck can I get some fucking health forms?" he asked her with a smile. She was shocked speechless.

Marlanna had been fearful of coming to the United States and even more fearful of working in an environment as strange and seemingly hostile as the securities business. She was sure there would be someone trying to trip her up, and now her worst fear had come true. Here was one of those big bullies, singling her out for attack, trying to see if he could get away with pushing her around on her first job in America.

Marlanna had been raised in a strict family, where pride of place and code of conduct were emphasized, and where even mild cursing was not tolerated. She was not about to endure disrespect by someone who was not even her boss.

Marlanna called the woman who had taken her employment application and asked what to do. The woman replied "I can't tell you what to do. It's up to you. Are you willing to file a formal complaint?" Marlanna hesitated. "Perhaps I should wait?" she said.

A few days later Marlanna's boss had a folder to be delivered to John. When Marlanna appeared at John's office, she was curious to see what kind of a person John had as a secretary. Rhonda was also an immigrant, although from a different country, and like Marlanna, her ramrod straight posture and highly proper grooming and diction gave off a no-nonsense air. While Marlanna was speaking with Rhonda, John's voice boomed out from inside his office.

"Rhonda, get your butt in here, and bring those fucking reports." Rhonda looked embarrassed and smiled sheepishly at Marlanna.

As Marlanna walked away she was incensed that anyone could get away with such blatant disrespect. She vowed to file a report if anything ever happened to her again.

Several weeks later John walked by Marlanna's desk in the morning and dumped a folder, not in her "In" box, but in the middle of her desk on top of her morning Danish. "Yeah," he said and walked away. Marlanna was livid, but said nothing.

Then that afternoon she was called into her boss's office and she took letters for an hour with the door closed. When she returned to her desk she found John sitting in her chair, with his feet up on her desk, smiling and talking on her phone. He continued talking while she stood by, fuming. At last she felt her anger rising up, and she slammed her pad on the desk. "Mister had better know I won't be puttin' up with this," she said. Then she stalked off to the employee complaint office and filled out a formal charge.

When the complaint reached John's ears he couldn't believe it. It alleged that he had singled out Marlanna for "harassment" and that his conduct was unbecoming an officer of the corporation. "You can't be serious," he told the company complaint handler. "I don't even know her name, for God's sake," he said. "I've never even spoken to her." And he added truthfully "What's this singling out crap? I treat everybody the same."

After the case was investigated John was found to have been "insensitive" and his actions were defined as "inappropriate." In another era he would have been told to "lay low" and Marlanna would eventually have been let go. But in the new era he was ordered to have a series of three sessions of "exploratory psychological consultations" at company expense to discuss his conduct. First, he was required to make a formal apology to Marlanna.

Playing a Game

John showed up late for our first meeting. He kept his coat on, sat down on the couch, crossed his arms and said "What's the drill?"

It was securities-speak for "what do we do here?" After hearing that the sessions were designed for open-ended discussion, he asked me if it was possible to "cut to the chase."

"I know how the game is played," he said. "I've been a bad boy and I get my wrist slapped. So let's get to the nuts and bolts and then I'm outta here," he said.

"Let's start with something about your background. Where are you from?" I asked.

"That's easy," said John. He enjoyed telling the story of his life, including the years at home in the family of four boys, the role of his grandfather and father as pioneers in the rapidly developing securities business, his legacy of maternal ancestors who had been movers and shakers for the past four hundred years, his triumphs on the athletic fields, and of course his rise through the ranks of the firm.

As an aside, he remarked that one of his boys was worrying him because he was getting "a nasty mouth." As the session drew to a close, John said "You mean that's all there is to this take `em out back to the woodshed stuff?"

"I don't know," I said. "You haven't told me what happened."

At the second session, John gave his account of the incident with Marlanna. He expressed his shock that anyone could take the whole thing seriously and swore that he would steer clear of her since she was a "potential psycho."

During the third session, I said, "We need to talk about noblesse oblige."

"What about it?"

"Whether you're aware of it or not, you're an aristocrat," I said. "Compared to other people in your firm, you're in the elite. Your family has been here for hundreds of years. That gives a person a very different outlook than someone who's been here for half a year."

"On my mother's side. Yeah, so what?" said John.

"There's more to it than that," I said. "You're an aristocrat on your own account, by some of your personal qualities."

"I am?" It was the first time John had dropped his pose of impatience and annoyance.

"You are. You are brighter and more gifted at business than most others. You are able to understand things in a moment that other people labor over. You have more natural energy and more ability to concentrate than the average bear. And you have more leadership qualities than most. You have a goal-directedness that is unusual. In all, you were intended to be quite the aristocrat."

John's face had a frozen look.

"But for the most part you don't act like an aristocrat. Your sense of noblesse oblige is poorly developed. Rather than having a sense of your station in life, that your native gifts have given you, and of the responsibilities these carry, you seem to have little concern or even awareness of the very people you could be showing the way."

"What do you mean?" said John.

"A man or woman with personal and life advantages can play a satisfying role in creating a better life for those around them. That's the premise behind the aristocrat."

"Why bother with somebody that low on the totem pole?" he asked.

"You might benefit by taking some time to look at yourself through the eyes of people lower down on the totem pole. Here's this big, tall, gruff-talking, fast-walking executive who knows everybody and has seen it all. He appears to be an over-powering force that bowls over everybody. To certain others you may seem like a force beyond reckoning, and a scary one at that."

John smiled.

"Maybe you've felt that way yourself...When was the last time you yourself felt puzzled and scared?" I asked.

John thought for a while and then his face clouded. "My dad," he said. "He blew in like a tornado, and he always left you feeling cut off at the knees."

"Yes. Well I'm sure you didn't like that very much."

John's face went blank. "It made me tougher," he said. "I got used to it."

He seemed to be remembering something and added, "At the end of the day, this lady is a loser."

"Could you define that? What's a loser?"

"You know, a loser. Somebody who's off the wall. A mental case, a psycho. Somebody who doesn't count." He paused.

"Marlanna doesn't count?"

"Well, no. Well, yeah. Yeah!"

"I think that's part of the problem. You have an inappropriate definition of the loser."

"So tell me, doc, what's a loser?" John was back to being sarcastic.

It was the end of the session. John agreed to come back for a half-hour continuation in a week's time, to complete the discussion.

Remarkably, he came on time and kept the appointment although it was no longer a requirement. And he repeated his question.

"So what's a loser?"

He added that he might as well have called Marlanna a "gook" or "creep." These were two other words John often used to describe people.

"Did you have any thoughts about it during the week?" I asked.

"Like I said, a loser doesn't count."

"I would say losers have lost contact with the areas where they can make a difference in their own life."

John shrugged. "So how else would you define a loser?"

"A loser is somebody who gets repeated chances to wake up about their role in making their own life what it is, but doesn't make anything from those chances. This episode with Marlanna is one for you. You'll be the loser if you don't realize anything from it; you'll be a winner if you can grow from it."

"Maybe," said John. He obviously wasn't convinced.

With the three sessions finished and the apology formally delivered, the episode was over.

The Nick Starts to Tighten and Then Closes

A year later, John was promoted to a much larger job in the company, managing a division with thousands of employees.

After some time on the job he took a major customer to lunch. The customer had known John's father and made an unflattering remark about the father's ruthless ways. John told the customer he was an "asshole" and a "geek."

The next day, the customer complained to the head of the company, threatened the removal of millions of dollars of financial investments, and demanded John's head on a platter. Had John not already alienated several other key customers, he might have weathered the storm. But as it was, John was demoted in part. He was placed in charge of a much smaller division although its emphasis on new technology made it important. The move was shuffled into the announcement of a larger corporate restructuring. And a second letter of reprimand was placed in his personnel file.

When Marlanna heard the story behind the events, she felt justified. "I knew the jake was marked for trouble," she said. "Imagine the man sittin' at my desk with his feet in my work."

John settled into the new job quickly. He told everyone he was doing "fabulous." In fact his bonus was as large as ever. He hired a crew of talented employees whose entrepreneurial spirit was compatible with his own. But trouble was brewing at home. One of his three boys began to get into serious "hot water" at school--it was the youngest boy, the one with a "fresh mouth," the one who was always getting into messy fights.

At home when John or the two older sons wrestled with the boy, the result was often tears, as his son tried mightily to defeat an overpowering force. John was worried that the boy might be, of all things, a cry baby, because John himself never cried like that when he was a boy. And John had always been able to handle his own fights without his parents being called in to school.

A year later John called me out of the blue. He rambled for a few moments about his problems with his son. Then he came to the point:

"I've been thinking about something you said."

"Would you like to make an appointment?" I asked.

"Nah," he said. "This business of being a loser. How would I know if my son was a loser?"

"Do you remember the definition of a loser?"

"Yeah. Somebody who messes up their own life and doesn't take responsibility for it."

"That's close enough."

"So were you trying to tell me I'm a loser?" John asked.

"Is that what you thought?"

"Nah," said John and without another word he hung up the phone.

The Chord of Fate is Cut

In the second session, the one where he described his family, it became clear that the main lesson John had learned in life came from his father. The lesson was never let yourself be a loser--someone who doesn't count. For his father, winning and losing were categories that applied at all times, to every form of human exchange. John was so far under the spell of this limited definition of life, of winning and losing as defined in terms familiar only to his family, that he couldn't see that Marlanna's difficult adjustment to a new country, and her bold and brave step into the complicated world of finance, were a form of winning too.

The unlivable dichotomy between winning and losing was the ruling premise of his life, and it became a tyrannizing force that alienated others and brought destruction into John's career and into his family.

What would have been necessary for John to overthrow the tyranny of always measuring life by "he counts" or "he doesn't count?" John would have needed to depose the "old world" of the male, as he knew it, in order to create a new world. It would have been equivalent to deposing his own father and grandfather, and the hundreds of years of ancestors who came before. It would have been the equivalent to saying that the premise of the past, however influential, "didn't count," that he was starting fresh. In the world of the male from which John came, this form of disloyalty was unthinkable and for John, unachievable.

Instead John handed down this tyrannizing conception of life, by "recommending" the winner-loser premise to his sons. In this way he wrapped his sons in the family garment of fate. The legacy that John passed on had become negative and enmeshing, and made for an unbearable burden for one person: his youngest son.

This young man in particular was poisoned the most by the family attitudes. While John's career continued "fabulously," his son became more and more of a problem. John shouted at the boy that he was a "loser" when he was expelled from school. Unlike John, the boy seemed to be making his own attempt at deposing the old world of the male, even though he lacked the means.

After the expulsion, the young man was sent to a boarding academy to "straighten him out." Like John, he had a reckless streak. On an evening of heavy drinking he took a friend for a ride along country roads.

As usual he drove too fast. Both young men were killed instantly when the car smashed into a telephone pole at one hundred miles an hour.

Unlike John, this youngest son did not appear to have the native characteristics of the one who everyone looks up to as a leader. According to John, his son was too "sensitive," and was neither as strong as his brothers, nor as quick mentally, nor as cocky. From all this, it was inevitable that the boy would form the conclusion, in a way that he could only express through his way of living and dying, that he didn't count.

Meeting the meaningful issues that come our way is a task that we often take as an optional exercise. We often treat it as something we can do if we so choose, after we get on with the business of getting ahead and making a living. Since the lack of a soul dimension in his life appeared to be symptomless, John felt no call to pay any attention to it. This lack of symptoms was a grave symptom in itself.

For others, those not caught up in living the same way as John, it was easy to see the threads connecting his attitude to Marlanna and his attitude to his son. A co-worker remarked after the funeral that John did treat everyone the same: he treated Marlanna the same way he did his son.

Who is to say what would have happened if he had been able to grasp the meaning of his episode with Marlanna? Perhaps the fabric of events-to-come would have unraveled. Perhaps his relationship with his son might have changed, and perhaps his son might even have been spared. Perhaps it wasn't this episode but some other that represented his crucial chance to grasp the soul-level of life; wave after wave of such opportunities wash over each of us. If only John could have learned to serve the sacred premise of the "boss at work" by fulfilling his noblesse oblige, perhaps things might have turned out differently.

In the end, the opportunities to reflect and to awaken, opportunities that John missed in the specific and the aggregate, do illustrate that the price for a lack of contact with the soul can be so dear, so shockingly high, that nothing else compares.

Epilogue: The Nick Opens Again

More than ten years passed. My secretary booked an appointment for a man who said he knew me well, but did not want to give his name. It was John. He looked like half of his former self. His hair had turned grey although it was still slicked back in the style of the Wall Street traders. His shoulders slumped, his eyes were red, and his face was lined. His suit was still a costly bespoke London banker's grey.

He sat down on the couch and quickly threw the three pillows on the floor. He told me the story of his son's death, his wife's pill-taking and drinking, and the collapse of his home life. He had a short affair with, of all things, a secretary at his firm but that didn't last. He was going through the motions at work and had a drinking problem of his own.

He had been through a "terrible shock" he said. He had been "broken."

"I come back all the time…to whether I killed my son," he said. "Everyone tries to reassure me about it. I came back to see you because I know you won't bullshit me about it."

"You don't want me to absolve you?"

"I can get that at church."

"How might you be responsible for what happened with your son?"

"I was too hard on him," John said.

"You're sure of that?"

"Yes."

"So it was part of your son's fate that he had a father who was hard on him. And it's part of your fate that you had a son who died. All we can do is make meaning of such things."

"That's…" John looked up from staring at his feet. He was about to argue. "I was going to say that's bullshit," he said, "but I'm not that man anymore. I'm here for your opinion. What's your opinion? Did I kill him?"

"I don't know if you did or didn't. It's probably not the right question."

"What is the right question?"

"Can you carry that you were part of the story of his life, including being hard on him?"

"What do you mean 'carry'?"

"Know it, know that it had consequences, know that you aren't absolved from it, and with all that, still resolve to learn from it and go on."

"Why should I do that?"

"It would be a way of honoring your son's life. You could add some meaning to the tragedy."

He nodded his head up and down. "I get the drill," he said. Then he stood up. "Do you think it matters, to know if he would be alive if I had listened to you years ago?"

"I think what matters most is what you're free to do now."

He stretched and with a half-smile walked to the door. With his back turned, he said as he left "See ya buddy."

In his son's honor, John took a portion of his millions and created a foundation to help troubled young men. He found that troubled young men often listened to him despite the difference in years and background. His message to them was often about the role of choice and freedom in life. He left the securities business although he still drew a large income from previous deals. For many years I received a Christmas card from him. He always signed it "A recovering loser."

-Chapter Five-
"Can the Soul die?"
How do you undo a Family Curse?

Prologue

The phone rang. It was my old and beloved teacher Evelyn Gillette. She had been a treasured mentor and friend to several generations of students. For me and for them she embodied the wisdom of the older woman.

"David, I want to refer a woman who has talked about killing herself, but actually I don't think she's in danger of that...there's strength there and a lot of self-awareness. I'm very concerned that if she sees a physician they will hospitalize her and stuff her with drugs. That would set her back in a really bad way...it might destroy her. But I know you can help her."

"Evelyn I wasn't thinking of taking anyone new right now. Can I give you the name of a colleague, someone I have a lot of confidence in?"

"I'm sure you're busy, David, but this is someone very close to me...she is very special...she's like a daughter. And you know I've never had a daughter. Can you possibly find a way to see her?"

"I see. Perhaps I can. I have someone else who may be finishing. What's her name?

"Flora Jovana."

"What does she say is the problem?"

"There's something about a clock that talked to her. There's a preoccupation with Pascal too. She is so much a soul worth saving. I can't thank you enough."

"Evelyn! Saving a soul…!"

"Yes, I know, but I'm really sure we can help Flora. She is the daughter of my life."

Before She Came To Me

As an adult, Flora Jovana was described by an associate as "the Mozart of hydraulics." While this seemed like a very strange appellation, nevertheless it expressed some important truths about her talents.

Like Mozart who "heard" fully developed symphonies in his head, Flora had the gift of envisioning fully developed feats of engineering in her mind. Like Mozart, the gift arrived early in her life; at age nine Flora designed a water clock with a float, a rack and pinion system and an hour hand, made from parts she found discarded in the back of a plumbing supply store. The water clock was impressive and she received a blue ribbon "First in Show" in the science fair at her Blair County, Pennsylvania grade school, besting the entries of older students. A photograph of her, standing next to the exhibit and next to a faculty sponsor who had no role in her project, shows a very thin, fair-haired girl in a faded sun dress, squinting at the photographer with a quizzical expression.

The prize-winning exhibit was impressive but the specifications Flora had drawn up were truly astonishing. She had drawn three other water clock designs, all equally workable, all very carefully illustrated on large sheets of graph paper. The sheer abundance of Flora's vision of her project, and the masterful, even playful grasp of mechanical principles were indications that a talent was at work, a talent that was already remarkably developed but which should also be nurtured.

However, there was no one around to nurture it. Flora was an only child and her mother had died when she was an infant. She lived in a large old dilapidated house with her father, Steven, a taciturn handyman who traveled their rural county looking for odd jobs and seasonal work. He was often away for extended periods of time, and Flora was raised by a series of housekeepers whose children were her early playmates.

There were no other relatives to take her in hand. Her parents' nearest relatives were in Vojvodina in Serbia, and after several changes in government and then war, the exchange of letters between Flora's father and the old country stopped.

Nor was there anyone at school to nurture Flora's talents. Her science teachers were all men, and they were nonplused by her talent. They weren't used to a girl with mechanical talent, a girl whose classroom doodling consisted of designs for a water tower the size of the Great Pyramid of Egypt.

Flora spent a great deal of her time in the library, and the school librarians who might have "adopted" Flora if she had been a gifted poet or writer or perhaps even a promising lawyer or physician, were put off by Flora's requests for Engineering Quarterly and the Journal of Hydraulic Research. Their puzzlement came out as disapproval, particularly since she did not look the part of an engineer. She was thin and pretty with delicate features, her hair tied back with a plain rubber band but nevertheless seeming wind-blown, and that inquiring quizzical look. It was her bold questioning of adults that did not suit the librarians, although she was shy with her classmates.

After Flora's exhibit toured the state capitol and was returned to her, she set up the water clock near the extra-large bed in which she slept and read and drew. She watched, absorbed in daydreams and fantasies, as the rotary motion of the bevel gears, the worm gears, and the pinion was converted into the to-and-fro motion of the sliding toothed rack. From her daydreams she made sketches and drawings, fanciful creations of her own invention that were as different as they could be, except for one feature: they all contained water.

During junior high school Flora discovered Pascal, the great 17th century French philosopher and mathematician. Pascal's law, that pressure exerted on a liquid is transmitted evenly in all directions, was the basis of all hydraulic engineering that followed, although the implications of his work were not realized for 200 years. Pascal died at an early age, only 39, and his tragic end and ethereal face appealed to Flora.

Flora's talent did cause enough stir to result, upon her graduation, in her receiving a Rotary Club scholarship to a Normal School, where it was presumed she could learn to become an elementary school teacher of science.

At the school she was finally fortunate enough to meet up with someone capable of recognizing her talent: the Dean of Students, Miss Evelyn Gillette, a deeply compassionate older woman with a gift for encouraging the best in her students. She was intrigued by Flora's open and pretty face, the plain hand-me-down dresses Flora wore, and her serious demeanor. She invited Flora to her office to have tea and to discuss Flora's academic schedule. Gradually in the course of several other meetings and then frequent hours of drinking tea together, Miss Gillette gained Flora's confidence. She asked to see the sketches Flora described and was astonished at the creativity, the variety and the breathtaking detail of Flora's work.

After talking with Flora for some time, and hearing about her passion for engineering, it became clear to Miss Gillette that Flora was at the Normal School simply because she hadn't been offered any other opportunities. And it was also clear that Flora was not meant to be a teacher.

So Miss Gillette called a university administrator who like many others was a devoted and loyal former student, and arranged for Flora to receive a full scholarship to an engineering program with a national reputation. Once enrolled at the bustling university, Flora experienced a familiar form of disorientation for country dwellers: the huge university seemed exciting and overwhelming at the same time. In particular the library was a source of wonders.

In the engineering classes Flora was often the only girl. The professors as well as her fellow students discovered that Flora had the engineering equivalents of total recall and perfect pitch: she could look at a design briefly and reproduce it exactly even when years had passed. Despite this intimidating fact, Flora's open and welcoming face led several of the boys to approach her and ask her for a date. They were surprised to discover that she was eager to go out with them, but were taken aback that she wanted to talk shop during the date, and hardly seemed interested in them as romantic partners. She became the class "pet" and the boys treated her surprisingly well.

One professor in particular caught her interest: the one who taught the two-term sequence on fluid mechanics and hydraulics principles. When he realized that there was very little in his course that she did not already know, he arranged for her to have a tutorial. She was the one student who could absorb everything he had to teach and whose passion for the subject matched his own. In the course of the tutorial, the professor often found his own understanding surpassed by Flora's in her areas of special interest. "She is a demon," he told Miss Gillette. "Very sweet and nice but her talent is a demon."

During the whole of college Flora kept her private work to herself; only Miss Gillette had seen her creations. They exchanged letters and Flora poured out her confidences to Miss Gillette, her triumphs in class, her scientific enthusiasms, and often, her aching loneliness and sense of being a rather freakish "one of a kind."

Flora graduated early and was given a letter of reference by her hydraulics professor to a large civil engineering firm in Boston. The job was as an assistant, and her tasks were menial in comparison to her talent, but the salary was far more than Flora had ever dreamed of earning. She changed her wardrobe to smart suits and stylish boots.

In a short time her extraordinary gifts were known around the firm and she began an apprenticeship under one of the firm's most talented engineers. As a team Flora and her new boss made computer-aided models of construction and flow problems that were used in feasibility studies for the firm's projects. She was fascinated by pipelines, pumping systems, design and operational testing.

As her work was well-received, Flora's responsibilities increased and her hours at work began to stretch into evenings and weekends. She presented papers at several conferences and her work began to appear in scientific journals. Now in her mid-thirties, Flora was promoted to senior hydrologic engineer, and received a large increase in salary.

Despite the workload, in her free time Flora continued work on her own projects. Her interest was gradually leading away from hydraulics and into the hydrosphere itself, with its all-too-familiar problems of imbalance of organic nutrients, pollution, acid rain, and warming due to trapping of gases.

In particular Flora was concerned with models of the earth's total hydrologic cycle, the process by which water is moved and transformed from one source, or one form, to another. She applied for and received a foundation grant to take a leave of absence from her job. She began work on a major new theory, a new model for the flow of water.

Flora's professional interest, her basic approach to her work, was gripped by the possibility of a grand and encompassing theory, a unified theory of the hydrosphere. Like many scientists in other fields, she wanted to find the "core" entity, in this case the series of equations governing the chaotic flow of water, which would reveal nature's very fabric, and give form to the grand scheme of nature's distribution of water. She told Miss Gillette that uncovering this scheme would be the equivalent of peering into the mind of God.

The work went well and at the end of three years Flora's partially completed study was published to much acclaim. A new grant to continue her work was offered by a wealthy private foundation.

Flora was now nearing the end of her thirties. Two important events came one upon the other. First, Flora's work was nominated for a renowned international Hydraulic Engineering award, the very highest in her field. Then her father died of heart failure, leaving Flora without a known relative. As the congratulations on the nomination poured in from all over, Flora returned to her rural home for the first time in years to close her father's affairs and put her childhood home up for sale.

After the funeral, Flora was alone in the old house. In her old room, she sat down on the large bed and found the old water clock, still operational, facing her as it did many years before. The clock moved and she watched the gears rotating and turning one another. Sitting on her bed a dark and terrible stream of thoughts came to her, grotesque and terrifying thoughts, thoughts that carried the most destructive force that thought can bring, thoughts Flora knew she should not think alone.

In a panic, she called Miss Gillette who had retired some years before, and was now living on the West Coast, in Brookings in the so-called "banana belt" of Oregon where, in a micro-climate, palm trees grew near the unspoiled rain forest.

"I need to see you," Flora said, her voice trembling over the phone.

"Where are you?" asked Miss Gillette.

"Back home. Can I come and see you?"

"Of course, dear, but I'm an awfully long way away. Don't you want to talk? Is there something wrong?"

"No," said Flora. "I'll be on the first plane. I'll call you when I know when I'm arriving." There was a pause.

"Thank you so, so much," said Flora.

Flora arrived in Oregon the next day. It was sunny and warm as she stepped off the plane, but soon there was a misty rain.

Miss Gillette gave her a hug; the first hug Flora could remember receiving in a very long while.

They sat down to tea on Miss Gillette's vine-covered porch and Flora told the story of all that happened to her recently, including the death of her father. At last Flora mentioned the nomination for the award.

"When do they announce the winners?" asked Miss Gillette.

"Today," said Flora.

"My goodness, let's check the newspapers." Miss Gillette opened her newspaper and there on the front page of the business section was an article on the winners in different fields. "A study on the flow of water received this year's engineering award," read Miss Gillette, and then she had to fold the page to read the continued story. "My God, it's you," she said. "You've won."

"Yes," said Flora in a numb voice.

Miss Gillette put down the newspaper and looked at her. "What's wrong, hon?" she asked.

"I have something I need to think and I can't think it," said Flora.

"It's that bad?"

"If I have to think it, I'll have to kill myself."

Miss Gillette's face lost its color. "It's that bad?" she asked quietly.

"Yes," said Flora.

"But this prize?" asked Miss Gillette.

"The prize means nothing to me."

"Oh, I'm so sorry dear," said Miss Gillette. For the time, no more was said. Miss Gillette's discretion, which had enabled Flora to trust her years ago, was still very much in force.

After tea, Miss Gillette convinced Flora to stay for a few weeks because she "needed help in the garden." Flora planted flowering shrubs, tended roses, and with Miss Gillette as consultant, designed and built several very large flower beds with borders of pineapple and fan palms. Miss Gillette had much to impart to Flora about the names of the plants, their folklore, and their preferences for soil, drainage, light, and air.

During the course of their working in the sand and dirt, Flora was able to talk more of her suicidal impulses.

"I did have a plan," Flora said, in answer to Miss Gillette's question. There was a rope and a chair. "I just don't know what to do with how I feel. I feel so awful," she said. Then she reached out and hugged Miss Gillette.

"I'm so grateful to you," said Flora. "Because I was so alone." She was finally able to cry and did so freely for a long time. When she lifted up her head her glance fell on an extraordinarily beautiful flowering plant in full bloom.

"I know this. What's this one again?" asked Flora, through her tears.

"That's a Christmas cactus," said Miss Gillette. "It's an epiphyte, though nobody knows it as one because it's almost always potted."

"A cactus that's an epiphyte!"

"In the rain forest it grows on another plant or on an object for mechanical support, just like an orchid. It doesn't take nutrients from the other plant, just support."

Flora smiled and Miss Gillette smiled back.

The two weeks passed quickly and Flora was ready to return to her work.

On the last day, Miss Gillette and Flora shared their favorite tea of the moment, a tea that came in a beautiful silk pouch. Flora gave Miss Gillette a matched pin and earring set to wear with grey and blue suits. And there was something for Flora. "Here is the name of someone who can help you dear," Miss Gillette said. It was my card. "And I have a gift for you," she said.

The gift was a large basket, lined with twigs, in which Christmas cacti of different colors had been carefully arranged.

"Will you come back soon?" asked Miss Gillette.

"Oh yes," said Flora, and she gave Miss Gillette a tight hug. "I'm so very grateful to you," said Flora. "I owe my life to you."

The Beginning of the Work

Flora took the train from Boston to see me, the first of many such long train rides. It was a rainy evening in Manhattan and her smart tiger-striped raincoat and matching umbrella were dripping as she hung them on the back of the door in my office.

In her first session she was awkward and nervous but her hands moved in the air as she talked. Her Pennsylvania accent was noticeably flat. Many of her expressions, mostly when she was upset, came from what she called Pittsburgh English ("my face needs washed.").

She spent the time talking about Miss Gillette, about what a special person Miss Gillette was, and she described in detail Miss Gillette's spectacular garden. She also mentioned a fantasy of what life would have been like if she had been adopted by Miss Gillette.

In subsequent sessions Flora talked of her work and her career, of the unified theory, of the properties of water and how so many things, even basic things, were still unknown about the flow of water. After a number of these "introduction to hydraulics" sessions, she brought in a book she had been reading.

"This is Pascal's Pensees. I've been rereading it," she said. "Can I read you a passage?"

"I would prefer if you told me what it says," I said.

"No matter then, I know it by heart," Flora said.

"It is wrong that anyone should become attached to me even though they do so gladly and of their own accord. I should be misleading those in whom I aroused such a desire, for I am no one's goal nor have I the means of satisfying anyone. Am I not ready to die? Then the object of their attachment will die...they must not become attached to me, because they must devote their lives and efforts to pleasing God or seeking him."

Flora finished reciting and was silent.

"What do you make of this?" I asked.

"Now that I've said it out loud in front of you, it seems extreme to me. But I underlined it in junior high school and I've reread it many times," said Flora.

"You said Pascal lost his mother at an early age too, didn't you?" I asked.

"Yes, age three," said Flora.

"What is it that seems extreme to you now?"

"He once castigated his sister for giving hugs to her children," said Flora. "He thought it was morally wrong."

"Yet he's famous for saying the heart has its reasons of which reason knows nothing," I said.

"Yes."

There was a pause.

"In this passage, he seems to be saying he has no use for human love, doesn't he?" I said.

Flora's eyes widened. "Is that what it means?" she said. "I never saw it that way before." Flora was silent for the rest of the session. During the next session she barely said a word, and again at the next session she came in, sat down and stared out the window. The noise from the streets of Manhattan made the silence greater in the room. After many silent sessions, she started to talk again.

"I have to talk about Pascal," she said quietly.

Now the talk flowed rapidly and in all the sessions that followed Blaise Pascal was the subject of Flora's conversation. It seemed that Flora had been "caught" since high school by a sense of identity between herself and Pascal. As a young person she needed someone to feel "the same" with, and Pascal seemed very close: they shared the same interest in hydraulics, they both suffered the loss of the mother at an early age, and now it seemed they both had a problem with emotional attachments. In some ways, she said, Pascal's life seemed more real to her than her own.

But, as Flora discovered through following up her thoughts with me, the differences between them were instructive.

Flora was very aware that she had never had the "advantages" of Pascal, whose education was directed by his father at home according to the highest standards. Pascal's father imparted a passion for mathematics, and young Blaise was exposed to many of the most intellectually distinguished names of his era. Flora told me with an anxious and present-focused concern that he was isolated from boys his own age and spent his time with his two sisters, one of whom later renounced her talents for the sake of religion. This sister also played an important role in Pascal's own religious development; Flora sometimes imagined herself as a "third" sister, the one who could have cared for Blaise just as he needed, the one who could have known him best of all.

As I pointed out to her, although Pascal's environment and education promoted his genius, Pascal's home life was far from balanced, for it left him with distaste for human affection. In Pascal's family and his milieu, being precocious was highly valued in its own right, with all the distortion of the childhood personality that inevitably results. Pascal was often haughty and arrogant, and no doubt these qualities were worsened by his childhood education.

In our sessions we now drew repeated contrasts, as a way of separating Flora from her unhappy crush on Pascal, and a way of raising her awareness of her own nature. It was the famous "working through" to her individual nature. We "discovered" the fact that Flora had never had the "blessing" of adult interference in her mental development and that this fact turned out to be a saving grace. Flora was allowed to remain for a long time in a natural state, spending whole days playing in the wildflowers outside her childhood home with the washerwoman's children. The result was that something dormant and "unspoiled" stayed intact in Flora, like the germinating power of a spore that can come alive after a rain. A hug, Flora said, could make her feel like she was a flower opening in bloom.

The laborious process of disidentifying herself from Pascal's attitudes and his unhappiness was important because it meant a first attempt to view her own unhappiness from an objective perspective. And the differences now became more obvious to her. For example, Pascal counted among his friends and correspondents many aristocrats, worldly socialites and even royalty, as well as leading mathematicians and scientists of his day. And he was engaged in a famous and acrimonious dispute with the Jesuits.

With her single-minded dedication to her career, Flora had only a small although close and loyal circle of friends. But she had many acquaintances who wished her well, and she did not have anyone she counted as an enemy.

Nor was Flora the beneficiary of a religious vision. She yearned for an experience like the chief event in Pascal's adult life, a conversion experience that occurred when he was 31. The evening of November 23, 1654 was his night of personal revelation, a two-hour long rapture that he experienced as direct contact with God, and which stayed with him all the rest of his days. He wrote down his ecstatic experience of that evening on a piece of parchment that was found sewn into his clothing after his death. It included the sentences "Joy, joy, joy, tears of joy," and "The world forgotten, and everything except God."

Pascal's ecstasy was in contrast to his bleak and tragic vision of man's condition, his view of nature as corrupt, and his concern with the God who is "hidden" from man; it was Pascal who spoke like a twentieth century existentialist when he wrote: "the eternal silence of the infinite spaces frightens me." This too frightened Flora, especially the eternal silence of her lost and dead relatives, the family that could not be a family.

While these visions and thoughts of Pascal's haunted Flora (she knew them by heart in both French and English) the closest she came to a vision of her own was her search for a unifying theory, her fascination with equations that could express the complications of hydrospheric cycles.

One day after many such discussions, a great deal of which had been focused on her obsessive identification with Pascal, Flora asked a new question:

"Where does an interest in science come from?" she wanted to know.

"What do you think?"

"I know it's a matter of temperament that one person is interested in nature or mathematics, while another person isn't. But there must be something very important behind my interest in water."

The question indicated that Flora was now ready to begin applying to herself, and her exploration of her life interests, the same principle she was applying in her engineering work: the search for an "underlying" theory or a central dynamism which could be expressed in a set of "equations." In this case she was looking for a "personal" equation.

"What do you think that might be?"

"I'm not sure, but I know it involves my mother in some way or another," said Flora.

Flora had been reluctant to talk about her mother, and this was the first time she had brought up her mother in quite some time.

"What about your mother?"

"I've always felt there is a mystery about her and I wonder if that same mystery is connected with my work."

"Can you describe something of the mystery?"

"I don't know...there's always been something behind the motivation for me...to try to uncover the secrets of how water works. When I was younger I wanted to be able to explain it to my mother, as if it would clear up the mystery and fill up the void."

Here Flora was on complicated and dangerous ground. It would have been easy to "reduce" her interest in science--in matter--to nothing but a search for the lost mother. The very word "mater," or mother, is the etymological root of "matter." But this would have been dime store psychology, producing nothing but an empty conclusion, a neat formula with no vitality, no lasting power for transformation.

As Flora said, it would have been the equivalent of saying that the sole reason Pascal felt the emptiness of the infinite spaces, and every existentialist who followed, was because they had no mother. Further, she noted that it was true that there were other scientists with adequate mothering who also had a fascination with the "basic nature of matter" as the mystery of the universe.

"It's the fascination of the work," she said, "that's what drives me."

"The mind of God?"

"Yes, can you see now why that prize means nothing to me?" Flora interjected in the middle of this discussion. "That's not what I was going for, it's not what motivated me."

"And now something has interfered with that motivation?" I asked.

"Yes, but I can't tell you what it is," said Flora. Her face was filled with pain. "I feel cursed."

There had been no mention of a curse to this point but the suicidal thoughts were always present, hanging over every session and every dimension of our work together.

Deepening the Work. Encountering a Family Curse

"You mentioned a curse recently," I said in a session soon after. "Have you ever heard of a family curse?"

"Yes…well, no, what is that?"

"It's an unworkable attitude to life, an invisible baleful influence, a blight for those who live under its influence, and it gets handed down from one generation to another, in a very direct way."

"Do you think I have a family curse?" Flora asked. "And how would you know it?"

"You know it by its symptoms," I said. "Sometimes it's a sin of the fathers, as the Bible says, that gets visited on the children for three or four generations. But more often I find that it is something that wants to be known, or something wants to be lived, something important, that no one 'gets' for generations. One way to look at it is that it's a meaning, a very important meaning, that wants to come into this world but there has been no one to express it, no human container to hold onto the message, no consciousness to register it, and it so falls very heavily in the lap of a new generation whether they like it or not."

"What is the cure for a family curse?"

"I would say that the cure for a family curse is the slow and gradual correction of an unworkable attitude toward life."

"And what attitude is that in my case?"

"For now, it seems your task is to take up your place in the universe. That is the antidote to a family curse of feeling you are 'digging your grave as soon as you are born' as you quoted from Thoreau."

"What does that mean 'take up your place'?"

"Of course, we're speaking metaphorically or even anthropomorphically. So I would say the gift of life 'wants' to be received with a correct attitude. It wants us to be engaged with life, not disaffected by the passing of what we once knew, nor by the suffering and evil of the world. If members of our family take this disaffected or detached view of life, if they set themselves up as disappointed 'critics' of life itself, then we are in the position of needing to differentiate our own attitude from theirs. What you are being 'asked' for is loyalty, loyalty to the fact that life wants to be inhabited as fully as possible. That would be turning against the enactment of the curse."

"Does everyone have this problem?"

"Well, some people are too tangled up in life, and some not enough. And some have to deal with both."

"The work we've been doing, it's to get me engaged in life?"

"Yes, yes! That's a very good way of putting it."

Going into the Low Places and the Secret of the Clock

"As an adult I've never really thought much about what it meant to grow up without a mother," Flora said. It was a session some months later.

"And as a child?"

"As a child I thought about it all the time."

"What were your thoughts?"

"I talked with my mother, in my head you know. My mother was a nurse, and I always pictured her in her white uniform. We had pictures of her like that with my Dad."

"What did you talk about?"

"I told her about my projects, and about my plans. I sort of reported things to her. What was going on."

"And?"

"It went on until I was a teenager..." Flora's tone was flat and sad. "Sometimes I was very angry with her for dying on me...I suppose the main thing I feel about her now is how distant she is, how absent." Flora began to cry. "There is an emptiness, a void, in me because of her...because of her absence." Long silences followed. Once again, the trucks and the horns of the cars and the hissing of the radiator in the room became very noticeable.

"I know I have a 'mother wound' but knowing it doesn't help," she said. From her tears Flora looked up. "Is it possible to fill a total emptiness inside?" Sobs punctuated her words. "I don't know a thing about it."

"You're a scientist...how does water fill things up?" I asked.

"By filling up the low places first."

"Yes."

"What are the low places in me?" she asked.

"The places where you feel the lowest and the worst."

Flora grimaced. "So that's where I have to start?"

All the previous discussion had been groundwork for this difficult realization. Among other things it meant that a more difficult new phase was about to begin. This session had touched on material of profound importance to Flora; it also let her know what she was in for, exploring the low places, now that she was able to encompass herself in a new way.

But there was much to digest now before more exploration could go on, and so it was not unexpected that she let the subject of her mother drop for some weeks.

When she was ready, after seeming to be preoccupied once again with hydraulics, Flora brought her own problems to a head by mentioning once again that she had kept so many secrets.

"Secrets are the great 'separator'," I said. "Children often become aware of themselves as a person for the first time when they have their first secret."

"What does that mean?"

"It means that secrets have a central role in creating awareness and a separate identity."

Flora was thoughtful. "I've certainly had my secrets, haven't I?" she said.

In subsequent sessions it became clear that the list of Flora's secrets needed to be very carefully explored.

Among the secrets were her private books of sketches and drawings, her obsession with Pascal, her hunt for the basic patterns of nature, her conversations with her dead mother, her fantasies about being adopted by Miss Gillette, her overwhelming joy in gardening with Miss Gillette, and of course her despair and thoughts of ending her own life.

However there were still many more secrets that she had begun uncovering in her sessions, facts about herself that had been secret and unknown even, and especially, to her.

One of those secrets had arisen in relation to her talent, which she had experienced as so powerful that it had thrown the rest of her personality into a dynamic imbalance.

Through examining her own life, and comparing it to Pascal's, she discovered that there is a dynamism to talents, to interests and "strengths," which can possess us in an autonomous way, upsetting our balance and equilibrium. Flora was beginning to grapple with the fact that a prominent talent imposes the need for its integration into the rest of the personality, into the whole person.

She was now more able to discuss the price she had paid for the gift of being a "Mozart of hydraulics," including the price of the imbalance in her social life. In high school, college, and as a young adult there were many times when her creative ideas wouldn't "shut off," leaving her scribbling furiously to record them. It was painful that others around her seemed to be more carefree, preoccupied with distractions and entertainment.

As she realized, it was almost incorrect to say that she was `reliving' this pain because she hadn't really experienced it earlier; now she was experiencing the past for the first time.

This new capacity for experiencing the unfelt pain from the past led in turn to the ways she had paid the price of not having a mother. In session after session Flora expressed her yearning, her aching for her mother, and also for her father, even for the long-forgotten world of her European relatives, all of which were lost to her.

Spurred on by her wider capacity for expression, she came at last to the very lowest of the low: she said she wanted to discuss the feelings that had started to surface while she sat on her old bed in front of the water clock, after her father's funeral. "Since you brought it up," I said, "what was the message from the clock?"

Tears were streaming down Flora's face as she stared straight ahead. In a flat tone of voice she recited the first part of the words of the clock.

"Time has beaten you," the clock said. "The things which made life worth living have all been swallowed up by the past...A person like you, with no connections to their origins, with no relatives, has been cut loose from humanity, from your own soul...Now you will float alone in those infinite spaces...alone."

As Flora said, suicide seemed like the only escape from these dreadful clock thoughts with their crushing weight of feelings.

"These are the things that I need to talk about," Flora said.

Each session now was like an "hour on the rack" as she allowed the "clock feelings" to strike. They consisted of her experience of the primitive, raw and overpowering emotions of deprivation, loss and aloneness, of abandonment and helplessness, of anxiety and fear, and of bitterness, rage and anger. All of these feelings rotated through her and she became progressively more aware of what only the clock had "known."

In addition to her dormant capacity for affection, it now became clear there was something else in Flora that had stayed intact. She also had the potential for the conscious experiencing of the whole range of negative emotions. This too had lain "dormant" in Flora as she grew as a child and as she went about her work in her twenties and thirties. Now she was strong enough to feel the claim of these emotions on her life.

All of this made clear that the impulse to suicide that she had felt on her old bed was now something that she had to come to terms with on a daily basis. The desire to "give up" and "do herself in" now came to be a familiar daily experience instead of a shocking all-at-once revelation.

During this period it seemed to Flora that our work together had resulted in what she called a "deprovement." Although she was in fact in no danger of killing herself, nevertheless the feelings of suicidal despair rose up day in and day out.

"I feel like Pandora in reverse," she said during this time.

"How so?"

"Instead of letting everything bad get out, I feel like all the ugly and horrible things of the world are coming home to roost. They're all crawling and alive inside me."

"Do you know the whole story of Pandora?"

"That hope came out last?"

"Yes."

"But was it false hope or real hope?" she asked.

"That's for each of us to decide."

It seemed that among many other things fate had given her a task: living with, and coming to terms with, generations of despair. Flora complained that this task seemed like a burden far greater than is placed on others. "Why me?" she asked. Surrendering to the temptation of self-pity, now she cursed her life, her talent, her looks, and of course, Pascal.

In one of these sessions she said:

"Even the pleasure in work is ruined now." Then she cried.

With its tumultuous ups and downs, this period of exploration of her unhappiness continued with no apparent end in sight. At a point when it seemed her despair had "heated up to the highest possible temperature," as she put it, just when it seemed that she had no reason whatever to hope for anything at all, a vision of hope did come to her through an unexpected discovery of how she might be healed.

The Vision

Flora at last had a vision. She felt this vision was hers alone and so it eased her dependence on Pascal's visions. It was a discovery that altered her experience so completely that afterwards the exploration of all of her feelings, including suicidal feelings, became "bearable" to her.

As was so characteristic of her, Flora arrived at her discovery through her knowledge of engineering.

It seemed that the topic of the "void" in herself had been especially puzzling to Flora because the "void" had also been a scientific concern of Pascal's. Until Pascal's time, there had been a confusion between the concepts of a vacuum and a void. Only beginning in his era were human beings starting to draw a distinction between the two. In retrospect it is understandable why it was so difficult to grasp the difference between a relative vacuum caused by atmospheric pressure (i.e. by the weight of air) and, in great contrast, a total void (a nothingness) in which no forces are at play. Both concepts address the issue of emptiness but are nevertheless very different.

Flora's vision concerning her "inner void" came on a Saturday night when she was alone as usual in her Boston apartment.

She had prepared a meal for herself, she had watched a newscast, and she had spent some time weeping. The feelings of despair, the emptiness, and the pain were present as ever. By habit, she took to sketching and her hands drew a water pump. Its complicated mechanism was based on a vacuum, which was created by a compression pump.

Staring at what she had drawn, Flora was overcome with amazement. Her hands had known the "answer," and had drawn a picture of the very thing she had been needing to uncover.

Flora was stunned to realize that the factor that she had omitted in her experiencing of herself was the concept of "external pressure"--a factor that she worked with every day in her hydraulic calculations.

Her great realization was that her terrible emptiness was a vacuum, not a void. Staring at her sketch, she saw that there must be an unseen (hence secret) compressor operating in her, a forgotten or unknown mechanism that created the emptiness, just as a compressor or vacuum pump is needed to create a vacuum.

In Flora's case the "compressor" was the force of all the unlived experiences and emotions she had carried dormant within her, hers and her relatives, as well as her elaborate but immature philosophy, bits of which were picked up from Pascal and from the scientific materialism that so dominates modern life, and also many unexpressed longings and desires and fantasies; in short all the unknown and unexplored dimensions of her negative experience of the soul that had forced out her "emotional oxygen" and made suicide her only apparent escape from what had seemed like a "void."

All these things had been outside her experience of herself and of life and so formed the "compressor" or "external pressure" that kept her locked in a vacuum.

Her vision enabled her to experience that there might indeed be a cure for her: the cure would consist of relieving the pressure, letting up on the compressor. (In fact our work together had already accomplished much of this; through exploration and the pursuit of a new and more mature approach to life, she had, bit by bit, come to breathe more easily despite the heavy weight of her despair.)

"I need to know all about this compressor," she said. She hesitated. "How would you describe the compressor?" she asked.

"As I said before, it's an attitude. For example, we can't be in some kind of competition to 'beat' time, and we are mistaken if we feel 'defeated' by time. It's a cultural mistake to think so."

"It's a curse."

"Yes, very much so since there are other and more complete ways to live with our time on earth. Time completes things and makes them ripe. The philosophers and now the physicists tell us that time is a dynamic manifestation of how things move out of potential and become real. Time is definitely not empty. Time is the ripener. It's the medium, the fluid, in which life germinates. Your 'family compressor' took the opposite view."

It became clear that Flora's very personal vision had the advantage of enabling her to see her own psychological system in bold relief; it gave her a "miraculous" standpoint outside her previous awareness of herself. Like an astronaut glimpsing an earthrise from the moon, she could start to comprehend not just the chaos of her inner experience but also how she might look when viewed as a whole, from the "outside" as it were. At last she had a model for how she might fill up the emptiness, a new perspective on the purpose of her life, a perspective different from Pascal's.

Her ability to sustain hope for a different kind of life, a life with emotional satisfactions, had been sorely tested. Now she had a model or an overview of how her transformation might come about. A positive connection to the soul could now make an entry into her life.

Of course it was an overview, not the journey itself. She would gradually have to come to know and experience those parts of herself that played the unseen role of the compressor. Anything but gradual change was dangerous; decompression at all once could have led to disaster. A slow and gradual change in the atmospheric pressure she lived under would allow for a real change in her psychological state, without harm.

Nevertheless Flora was having her first experience of the ordering principle in her own psyche, an experience that is always awe-inspiring, something experienced as sacred or holy, as exceptionally meaningful. It was her own version of the most convincing experience an unhappy person can have: the birth of order and meaning from the very material experienced as most "me." The value of her own particulars, of her own specific nature, was a new premise for living.

Long before in Miss Gillette's garden, and now through her vision of her cure, Flora had seen what was possible for her in the midst of her emptiness. These "brief glimpses of ecstasy" as she called them, kept her going during the rough hours and days that were ahead. They were a first "blossoming" of her personality that was neither false nor entirely real and permanent. As Flora said, the healing glimpses of ecstasy were "gifts" that gave her the courage to hang on: "Now that I realize I actually do have a psychological system, I'm not as frightened anymore," she said. "It was living in chaos that nearly did me in."

Engaging in Life

For the next period of time, Flora explored the ways in which she herself had structured her experience of life: her withdrawal into the world of engineering, into long hours of work, and the distance she set up between herself and others to protect herself from more loss and hurt and unbearable disappointment. It gradually became clear that there was a series of walls-within-walls she had built, which protected her but kept her isolated from her own experience and from closeness to others.

Her father was also much on her mind. She realized how much sadness he too had held in over the death of her mother, how the burden of despair she felt was also a legacy of her father's brooding and inward ways.

Digging in his effects, she found the old letters from his relatives in Europe. Acquainting herself with people long since dead, she was able to see that a strain of melancholic disaffection with life was also part of her familial inheritance for generations into the past, a burden that came down to her as well as to her father. "There is such a thing as the Slavic soul," she said. Then she added, "But you don't have to be Slavic to have a family history of despair."

During this time she found a letter of her father's. It had been written a year after her mother's death and was marked "return to sender." He had written to his family, expressing his powerful grief over his wife's death, and his wrenching concern for his motherless daughter, and the terrible thoughts of doing himself in that he was fighting every day, fighting solely because of his sense of obligation to his child. The message had not even been able to reach the relatives. As Flora said, the letter was now a message from the grave that enabled her to see her father in human terms. Her new perspective on his life helped to clear up much of the puzzle of his appearing to have had no inner life, no emotional life, just as once she had thought she had none.

A still-deeper understanding of the motivation for her thoughts about suicide came during this period of discussing the "internal void." She began to realize that it was not just an escape from pain that had made suicide so tempting. Even in her very worst moments, she had never given up on her glimpses of "ecstasy" but she had assumed they could be found by ending life. It was more than sobering, it was downright shocking, to discover this meant she had projected "ecstasy" onto death.

As a consequence of all this new understanding of herself and her origins, Flora began to see others more clearly. In a session during this period she said "in the past few months, men seem to have just come out of the haze. I don't think I ever really saw them before." She began dating ("nothing serious as yet") and went about filling up her free time with activities with friends.

The subject of her award came up again. Before, Flora had dismissed the honor, saying: "That's not what I was in it for." Now she was ready to face the fact that she did care about the award. After all, as she said, it represented the pinnacle of success in her field and was awarded for her long years of hard work.

Back then, because she felt so empty inside, there was a huge gulf between her "actual" despairing experience of life and the "ideal" status of having won such an award. The gulf between the two was too much to bear. In order to go on, she had to eliminate the importance of one and there was no question of which it would be. At the time, the premise behind her despair was far more potent than experiences like winning the award.

Now, it was especially painful for Flora to realize that she had missed out on a pleasurable and rewarding experience, an experience of connecting to others and the world, by skipping the pomp and circumstance, the "strokes," that went with the award ceremonies, which were held in Europe. An once-in-a-lifetime opportunity had seemingly been lost.

It seemed too much to hope for, but now a "second chance" arose. Flora received an invitation to a large formal reception for all the American winners of the prize, past and present, to be held in Washington, D.C.

"Do you think I should go to the reception?" she asked in her next session.

"What do you think is at stake?" I asked.

"I could just blow the whole thing off, and they would chalk it up to the 'reclusive scientist' bit," she said.

"Wasn't your study a real contribution...to the overall understanding of the hydrosphere?"

Flora seemed to squirm. "Of course it's not the last word. What I've done so far is not even really an introduction." She was about to launch into the details of what still needed to be done.

"If you won't make a place for rewards, for the recognition of your peers, then you've really placed yourself out in those 'infinite spaces,' haven't you?"

Flora grimaced. "I'm doing it again, aren't I?"

Flora decided that she finally had a use for some of the money she had saved over the years: she bought an exceptionally expensive red Valentino dress. In Washington she hired a limo to take her and a group of friends to the reception. On her return she said "It's possible to drink more champagne than I had imagined...I didn't feel my feet under me for the whole evening. I got invitations to dinner parties from people I'd never met before! One of the hostesses told me there was a senator who wants my phone number." She giggled. "It seems silly but it was fun."

While the improvements in her life were now something that she herself was able to feel and describe, there was a final topic waiting before her work with me would draw to a close.

"How are all these things perpetuated, what keeps a compressor going like this, years later?" she wanted to know.

"Fundamentally, it's an attitude toward life," I said.

"Which part do you mean?"

"For one thing, your attitude has been that things can be compared."

"When did I do that?" she said. Smiling, she added "Besides Pascal."

"Good question."

Of course Flora had compared herself to Pascal. But she had also compared her personal life to her professional life, especially around the issue of the prize, and with devastating results. She compared the second part of her life to the first, her adult life to her childhood. She compared her present life to the "ideal" life she imagined, a life with a large and happy extended family. And of course she compared herself to others who appeared to have no burden of talent.

"The problem with comparing is that it compresses the uniqueness of things," I said. "There never has been a Flora before, nor will there ever be a person like you again. No one else can feel things exactly as you do, no one can see things as you do."

Flora sat thinking for a long while.

"Is 'uniqueness' what fills the emptiness?" she asked.

"I would say yes. If we can grasp how each of us is new, how each of us has never been tried before in God's and nature's Grand Experiment, then we live close to the way life flows, in balance and close to the soul."

"Then comparing is a distorted hypothesis?"

"Oh yes."

"This really has broad effects?"

"Definitely."

"And experiencing the uniqueness of things, keeping them separate...could we call that a core entity, an equation at the center of life?"

"Most definitely."

"I feel privileged to know of it."

"Yes."

"It's really an honor to know about this, isn't it?"

"Yes."

The Final Encounter with the Clock. Can the Soul die?

In the last period of our work together, Flora was engaged in making her definitive evaluation of Pascal; she said she was ready to bury someone who had been dead three hundred years. Like a teenage girl who believes a rock song lyric was written specifically for her, Flora's self-referential approach to Pascal had been both a symptom and a cause of her ills.

According to Flora, Pascal needed to accept not only the God who could be experienced in an ecstatic vision but also the God who was present in the smallest expression of affection. Her own task had been to learn not to compare the two. She decided that Pascal didn't realize he was rejecting God and the soul when he criticized those hugs meant for the children.

Flora was freeing herself at last from the tyranny of the least differentiated aspect of Pascal's philosophy, of his view of God as separate from all the things in the creation and therefore hidden. As a result she was no longer experiencing herself as completely separate from life.

Now at long last the most destructive, terrible and unnamable thoughts which came to her while watching the water clock after her father's funeral were ready to move out of the realm of secrets.

In a session filled with many silences, Flora finally shared the whole of her burden, the remainder of those frightening and horrifying words.

In the same flat voice, the special voice for telling painful things, she said:

"I can tell you now the last clock thoughts."

I nodded.

You have no place in the creation, in the universe, you will live and suffer in a void, like the death of your unknown mother and your forgotten father. Your subjective existence will die with you and all of memory of you will be destroyed. Your soul will die, unknown and extinguished. Nothing of you will remain, nothing, nothing."

This was the last and final statement of the clock, expressing a point of view that was the epitome of darkness—a sign that Flora had reached the bottom of her darkest thoughts. There was nothing darker and more dreadful. I noted to myself that it was also a sign of health that this ultimate darkness could finally be shared between us.

"Can a soul die?" she asked. "Is what the clock said actually true? I was almost convinced and I was ready to kill myself. I really don't know, I don't know, I don't know." This was heartbreaking to say, and to hear. "Can you tell me what you think?"

"I don't know either," I said. "I don't know how anyone could know for certain. But I do know that if we live thinking that even the soul perishes, that will spoil our enjoyment of life while we have it. And if we live with some sense of a principle operating behind this life or beyond this life, the greater life of the soul, then we can better enjoy this life."

"Can you say it again?"

"If we feel something lasting in ourselves, and in our connection to others, then we are able to inhabit our lives better. We're able to pursue our work and our relationships with a quality of aliveness. It's purely a matter of living creatively with a mystery. I like to think our soul walks out of space and time when we die, and into another boundary circle, with a very different horizon."

"Like inside a black hole?"

"Who knows what happens in a black hole? From there it seems almost nothing is reachable in this world, but who knows? If we don't think or feel something is eternal, we are alienated from ourselves and the flow of life. And yet we can't diminish the importance of this life on behalf of an eternal one either. Those thoughts are what I have to content myself with."

"Are you saying that the eternal things are a valid experience, even though they aren't a scientific fact?"

"Oh, I like that! That's very well said!"

In the next period of our work together we discussed the nature of darkness and despair, and how time itself had come to carry these dimensions for Flora.

I introduced the idea that time has been seen in some cultures like our own, as linear and irreversible, while in other cultures time is cyclical and the essential things are never lost. Time is the devourer but also the creator; for some cultures time is a divine mystery worthy of being called a god, a god who sends forth life in a flow like a river of time.

We discussed how a true (that is more complete) understanding of a clock is that it measures the human dimension of time while also pointing to the divine mystery of time's unending quantity and quality, and so a purely mechanical and mechanistic view of clocks and time is one-sided and imbalanced.

"How a person views time will determine how they view their own life and how they experience their own life," she said.

"That is so true," I said.

The final phase of our work seemed to be an extensive discussion of time, but of course it was not really about time but about Flora.

"If time is nothing but a devourer then all we see is time's dark side," I said. "That side is no doubt real and inescapable but if we focus only on that side, we are out of balance. The creative side of time, that nothing becomes real until it steps in to time and that time is the medium by which and through which creative acts can be born, that side of time needs to balance our recognition of the truth that time has its dark side."

No one in Flora's family could bear the tension of standing in the middle, facing the reality of the darkness but still holding onto the light. That was the family curse and it had many negative effects. The curse greatly inhibited the bonds of affection that had never been adequately formed for generations of her family. These negative effects of the family curse perpetuated themselves with a vengeance.

"This curse is very strong," Flora said. "It isn't weakened by passing from one generation to another."

"Yes, it's very strong."

"How can I exorcise it?"

"You have to know what it wants."

"What do you mean?"

"A family curse 'wants' to be resolved by approaching it positively as an unfulfilled desire."

"What desire is that?"

"It seems the curse wants light and warmth and human closeness. These have dispelled it, and these will dispel it."

With her brave investigation of the curse, the first and only such investigation in the multiple generational lives of the curse, its energy was weakening and draining off. The closeness Flora was able to achieve with Miss Gillette was part of what broke the curse, along with the raising to consciousness within Flora of the nature and effects of the curse itself— the curse could only perpetuate itself in darkness. These were realizations that wanted, with a mighty desire, to "live" and to be "embodied." The realizations required a higher level of consciousness that could only be achieved in the form of awareness by one individual at a specific moment in time. Flora had risen to that level as the pioneer in her family history, the first to do so.

"I have a quote for you," she said. "It's from Lord Byron:
"There is that within me…that will breathe when I expire."

She added "What a thought! And what if the thought was an experience? An experience like that might make life very different…a personal fact but not a provable fact."

All these new discoveries led to a round of work in our discussions on her attitude to her gifts, and how she needed to accept her wonderful talents for engineering with a grateful acknowledgment that they were indeed gifts. In this new round of work she was beginning to comprehend how much energy she would have to devote to make sure she herself would benefit from those gifts, and not be their "victim."

"I'm still wondering what it means that people said I was a Mozart," she asked.

"Mozart gave glorious music to the world but his gifts didn't benefit him personally in the same measure," I said.

"He was buried in a pauper's grave," Flora added.

"In some way we are all dealing with the Mozart question...in the sense that we all need to get the benefit for ourselves from what gifts we are given."

"How do we do that?" she asked.

"By making sure the expression of our gifts passes through the field of our awareness. If Mozart had done that, it's almost certain that he wouldn't have written some glorious symphony or another because he would have been busy taking better care of himself. It would have been our loss, but his gain."

"Does it always have to be that way? Pitting the benefit of the individual against the benefit of the society?"

"No, definitely not. But the world at large isn't organized around whether Mozart has a fulfilling life, it just benefits from his music. Only Mozart can be concerned with managing his own life. In his case, as in yours, that means placing these gifts in the context of your whole life, instead of the other way around."

"What do you mean, the other way around?"

"It's the tail wagging the dog if you allow your gifts to dictate the rest of your life. Again, it may benefit the rest of the world, but not you."

"So that's why the award didn't mean anything to me...at the time." She added thoughtfully "you're talking about a way of living life that's inclusive...it's more than making scientific discoveries, without making them into any less...although that's all I would have asked of my career before."

"Yes," I said. "You might think of this as a core entity in those life equations you've talked about. A life equation includes a place for the value of your own soul along with the value of your gifts."

Closure

The last major remaining task in our work together now eased itself into view, ready to be tackled because the ground had been prepared for it. As our work neared its end, there was an important "closure" task for Flora. This task consisted of becoming more aware of the dimensions in which she was now a profoundly different person. Although, as she noted, there might be others who would not find her that different. After all she still lived in the same apartment in Boston, continued work on the same projects, and followed many of the same routines in her daily life.

She was now assimilating the fact that the healthy part of her personality was able to generate a pressure and an atmosphere of its own, a "healthy" pressure. The power and the energy in the compressor had not escaped into the "infinite spaces." The energy that had been trapped in those negative "clock" images was now available in a new form. It had been transformed into a new vitality in her daily living, in which she could experience her life and her work as full of life and motion instead of successful but empty.

She was able to summarize a great deal of our work together.

"I think I was caught in a paradox," she said. "The clock said I was separated from my family, but the curse kept me too much in the family."

"That's very well said."

"You can synchronize an inner clock with the outer clock," she said.

This encompassing realization was more than an "insight." It was a lasting realization that Flora now embodied in her whole person.

The profound difference in Flora extended to a new dynamism for relationships, a capacity for "making things bloom" with a few select people. Previously she had been afraid she would be unable to live in the "pressure cooker" of a relationship. Now she began dating one man regularly. For some years she had been spending vacations in Oregon at Miss Gillette's home. Awkward but elated, she now brought her steady "beau" to meet Miss Gillette.

Walking hand in hand with her companion, Flora returned to Miss Gillette's garden and showed off the roses and perennials she had planted. She laughed when her companion was curious about the spectacular epiphytes ("you have these in your apartment too," he said) that had played a central role in her transition to a more soulful way of living. They had been a symbol for her of how she could be able to "attach" herself to another person without either person giving up essential parts of their selves. Even the "banana belt" of Oregon had become a symbol for her of a more "temperate" way of living, a temperate zone where things could flourish in a mild climate.

On these return visits she was always astonished to see how what she had planted had taken hold so vigorously, and had spread into shapes and sizes that were far removed from the small seedlings that she had planted. The same could be said for her: by encountering her inner world, she had set in motion a process of growth in herself that was now able to flow and to generate life on its own.

Epilogue

A year later, Flora and her beau were married in Miss Gillette's garden. Miss Gillette wore a shimmering light blue suit she had the tailor make for the occasion, to go with the pin and earrings that Flora had given her.

Three years later, Evelyn Gillette died in old age and left her beautiful home and her estate to Flora.

On the day after their wedding, I received another call from Evelyn Gillette.

"So was I right...did we save her soul, David?" she asked me.

"We did do something extraordinary for sure Evelyn...although that's not how I think of what we did," I said.

"What did we do?"

"I think both of us, you and I, we did what people can do for each other. We invoked the soul-saving function of her psyche, you with your amazing love and caring, and me with my devotion to the work, and then the healing power showed up within her and did the saving."

"It's a great mystery isn't it?"

"Oh my God, is it ever."

-Chapter Six-
"I Want My Career To Be My Statement To Eternity."
How the Soul Can Help Us to Keep a Pact with What's Important

As we get older, the great danger is that rather than solidifying our relationship to the soul, our hidebound attitudes can petrify us. This is the story of a woman who was convinced her life was over in all essential aspects once she lost her job. Instead she was presented with the fact that the soul challenges us to grow at all ages.

The Flame Is Lit and then Burns Out

Jane Covantrie was appointed to a job she called "keeper of the sacred flame" at her company when she was in her late thirties. In this new exalted position, the secrets that were entrusted to her carried a powerful charge of excitement and energy, which Jane felt surging through her every two weeks.

To others the job might have seemed a bit more mundane. Jane was put in charge of recordkeeping for the personal accounts of the senior officers of her accounting firm at a fashionable address on Park Avenue in New York City. She kept records of all the personal financial dealings of the senior officers: paychecks, stock grants, options and bonuses, as well as their retirement accounts.

Every two weeks on payday, a courier arrived in Jane's office carrying a black leather pouch. He brought confidential materials that were produced in a back office downtown. The black pouch contained the pay envelopes for the senior officers, including one black-on-green check made out to the chairman in the staggering amount of $26,000. After initialing her receipt for the pouch and logging its contents in an entry book, Jane was ready to begin what she called her "walk," the trip with pouch and envelopes in hand through long plush carpeted corridors to the offices of the senior executives.

Small, fine featured and slight, with her prematurely grey hair held into a severe-looking bun by a crocheted black lace net, Jane dressed very conservatively and wore simple gold earrings and a single strand of pearls. Her ensemble matched the pouch.

Jane worked in a remote location but on the same floor as the senior officers. Her area was called the "outer sanctum" to distinguish it from the "inner sanctum" of the senior executives, who were called "the gods" in the colloquial language of the employees. The women who worked in the outer sanctum, many of whom looked and dressed like Jane, were called the "nuns." In the company lingo, each of the employees had a "world" as in "Jane's world is recordkeeping." If an action or decision was of a scope far greater than an employee's "world," it was said that the decision needed to be made "at the level of the gods."

This impression of scope and power was greatly desired by the company. Its resources were enormous and the offices of its several dozen subsidiaries extended around the world. Every day important visitors came up from the vast marble lobby in a private elevator to the senior executive suite and were greeted by uniformed guards who wore white gloves. Standing next to the guards were three young men in blue blazers with the company logo in gold on the lapel. They were floor guides, and they also wore white gloves. The sole function of the guides was to accompany visitors down the long corridors that led to the offices of the senior executives. The floor guides were instructed not to speak with the visitors unless spoken to first.

Impressed as she was by the size and power of the company, the hair on Jane's neck never failed to tingle as she walked, hushed and reverential, down the long corridors with their deep-blue velvety carpeting, gilt-edged paneling and elaborately framed paintings from the company's private art collection. She handed off the last check with a sense of "mission accomplished" that made biweekly Fridays the highlight of her work life.

The exciting element of secrecy entered into Jane's work because she knew how much each of the important people got paid. On the one hand, this information was available to anyone who was curious, in the pages "Annual Compensation, Office of the Chairman" of the company's annual report. On the other hand, the exact amount of the biweekly paychecks for the senior officers was perhaps the greatest secret in an environment where all kinds of information and data were kept secret on principle, whether there was a rationale or not.

As a result Jane was deeply impressed with the grave responsibility arising from the extreme confidentiality of her job. As she walked through the long corridors, she wore a slight but airy smile, confident that in her role as guardian of financial secrets she had received a special dispensation from above.

Naturally her secrets kept her somewhat isolated from the rest of the company. For example, the chairman himself would call her and ask: "Jane, could you be a dear and calculate the dividend on my restricted shares?"

And even though the information would be officially tabulated and distributed in just a week's time, Jane would make new calculations and give an immediate update. When she called him back the chairman was both gracious and grateful: "Jane, what would I do without you?" he asked rhetorically. "You're a treasure."

Then, instead of being able to share the rather exciting news that the chairman had called her himself--not his assistant--and that, even more, he had been most laudatory, Jane simply went to the glass-walled Bauhaus-style lunch room and sat down with her colleagues and smiled quietly while the conversation and the gossip flowed on.

In this way many years passed and the chairman retired. But the new chairman had also spent his years at the company with Jane as his financial records-keeper. He too was appreciative of the efficient way that Jane kept track of his accounts.

During her thirty years with the company, Jane remained single. Her needs were simple, and just as she carefully managed the accounts of the senior officers, she was careful and tidy about her own monies. She felt lucky to have so much of her life in order, and most grateful to the company for the opportunity to serve in such a trusted and valued capacity.

Then, as in the Bible, there arose a "new Pharaoh over Egypt who knew Joseph not." In this case, the new Pharaoh was a chairman who was brought in from another industry, a man whose compensation had been negotiated in secret by the members of the board of directors. Jane and her records had not been consulted.

The new chairman brought with him a team of his own assistants. One of them had the responsibility for handling the personal accounts. In a short time, everything that Jane had done before by hand was automated and available on the company's intranet. Jane sat for several months in her office with almost nothing to do. She no longer took her "walks" every other Friday. She was sure some oversight had resulted in her lack of participation in the transfer of power, but she was confident that the situation would be corrected. After all, she was still receiving occasional account inquiries from senior officers from the old team.

Then one day Jane received a notice in the mail, indicating that her job had been eliminated. The notice was two paragraphs long. The second paragraph indicated that she had two weeks to complete the transfer of her work. It was signed by one of the new assistants to the chairman.

Jane was speechless with shock and anger, and began to shake at her desk. For a few minutes she sat in a daze, unable to move. Then, with her voice cracking from emotion, she dialed the number of the previous chairman. His secretary was wise enough to recognize Jane's in extremis state, and put her through immediately. The ex-chairman was disturbed to hear of this development and said that of course he had not been consulted.

He asked Jane to stay by the phone while he made some calls. Unfortunately, it turned out that the new chairman was away on a business trip and was unreachable. One of his aides indicated that the elimination of Jane's job had been reviewed according to company policy and that there was nothing irregular to report. The ex-chairman wasn't satisfied. He asked for a return call from his successor and the matter was set aside for the day.

Jane was grateful to hear that the ex-chairman had been on the phone on her behalf. She was still at least partly convinced that a terrible mistake had been made, and she agreed to wait until the next day for some form of response. She took the train home to her small house in Connecticut, and immediately got under the covers after taking a sleeping pill.

The next day was a Friday. Jane heard nothing from anyone, and at the end of the day she called the ex-chairman's office. He had already departed for an engagement, and his secretary reported that he had not received any calls from the new chairman.

Jane spent the weekend in a haze. She had always taken a mild tranquilizer during stressful times, but never more than one a day. Now she took the pills as often as the dosage allowed, and still she found herself shaking whenever her thoughts drifted back to what had happened.

Despite the pills, for the first time in many years Jane found herself longing for her mother. Jane's mother had been her closest companion, her one true friend. Jane's father had died when she was a teenager, and her mother had been everything to Jane. Together they shared all of

Jane's college years, and they continued to live together as Jane went out into the world of work. Every evening they ate dinner together and relived the events of the day. When Jane spoke of her mother she always used the phrase "my sainted mother."

But her mother had been gone for many years and although Jane thought of her every day, she had not experienced the longing for her mother with such intensity since the year of her mother's death. The grief then had been overwhelming to Jane. Now it seemed as if the intervening years, and the healing of the open wound, had never occurred. The experience was as confusing as it was painful, because Jane didn't know if this meant that she was losing her grip on things, losing her actual sanity.

On Monday she went to work and received a call from the ex-chairman. He was sad to say that there was nothing he could do to change the facts of the matter, although he offered to help Jane find a new position. "Have them call me," he said, "and I'll give you the best damned reference there is."

At work that day several people stopped by her office to offer their condolences. Jane found their visits painful, because she was still shaking so much. She was fighting a losing battle to keep her emotions in control.

After writing detailed notes and instructions on all of her files, Jane called in to work and said she would be taking some of her long-postponed vacation time in place of her final two weeks.

She went home, locked the door and sat down on her sofa. The sofa now became the focus of her life. She got up only to check the mail, to go shopping for food, to bathe and to go to bed. Days passed as she sat on the sofa.

For the first time in many years, Jane didn't get dressed for church on Sunday. She had been active on various committees and had served as financial record keeper for many social events. When she was missed, and people from church called, she told them "I'm fine, but I can't talk right now." When the minister called, she was tempted to tell him that if she was away from the sofa for too long, she began to feel near to panic. But instead she told him she couldn't talk because she had something on the stove.

The long hours spent alone gradually began to wear away the edges of her everyday personality. When her prescription for tranquilizers needed refilling, Jane took a walk early one evening down the tree-lined streets of her small suburban town. For the first time she noticed that her hearing had changed. She was hearing things in the foreground, noises and conversation, as if it was in the background. And the background noises, the wind in the trees and the drone of a far-off airplane, were in the foreground.

After weeks of nearly total isolation, Jane woke up from a pill-induced sleep and realized she had been sobbing in her dreams. Now that she was awake the sobbing continued so uncontrollably that Jane seemed to herself to pass out. When she awoke, her face was lying on a wet pillow. She got up and walked toward the linen closet to get a fresh pillow case and her knees buckled. She lay face down on the floor as the sobbing came back once again.

It was an emptying. Jane was emptying her grief, and something even more essential, and when it seemed as if there couldn't possibly be anymore emptying, then the noises in the background began again to assume loud proportions, and the sobbing came again and brought Jane to her knees time and again. When she was worn out, she made her way to the sofa and sat.

After several months of this self-imposed isolation, the ex-chairman called with news of a job opening at a company run by one of his neighbors. Despite the shell shock of the previous months, Jane put on her interview suit and went to see the chairman's contact. The contact proved to be another "gentleman from the old school," a man rather like the ex-chairman himself, who could appreciate Jane's serious demeanor and obvious professional qualities. He told her the job was hers, provided that she was willing to accept a reduction in pay of 25%.

Since money was not an issue, she accepted the job and began work. Her new employer was impressed with the polite and gracious way in which she went about her business.

Soon Jane fell into a routine again and the feelings of grief and despair began to recede. Two weeks into the job, she stopped taking the tranquilizers during the evening. It was a relief to be tired enough to sleep.

Her new colleagues found her pleasant enough, if somewhat guarded, and they accepted her without much fuss.

Jane's work was quite similar to her old position, except that the accounts at the new company didn't have many of the features that had been introduced at the old company. Despite her attachment to the "old ways," Jane was familiar with new accounting practices and could operate the necessary software programs. Her suggestions for improvements were well-received by her new employer and Jane began to find her new position "homey."

Then the impossible happened. Her boss was moved out, a new man took over, and Jane was let go again. This time she was able to laugh a bit about it, even though she was shaking once again. She resolved not to go through the same tortuous experience of isolation again and began to send her resume to her old contacts among the senior executives.

Once again she found an opening on her first interview, and she started work at her third company in less than a year. But something was different this time. Jane found the work unsatisfying, and she became frightened when the background sounds at work--the ringing of telephones, the voices in cubicles nearby, and the hum of the copying machine--started to become overly noticeable again. At night the sofa seemed to compel her to sit again.

It was at this point that her physician decided she needed something more than tranquilizers. Jane was reluctant to take any of his referrals, but eventually she called me.

Making a Beginning from Foolishness

In our first session Jane sat with her hands on top of the large black clasp purse on her lap. She looked around the office and nodded appreciatively. "I like Matisse too," she said. She was quite reserved and described her problems (including the hearing problem), with a slight laugh, as arising from the "infirmities of crossing the Rubicon of seventy years of age."

In the second session I asked her to tell something of her family life.

"My mother, my sainted mother," she began, and then the sobbing started. Jane wept for the full session and many more. At the end of one of these sessions she said:

"You must think I'm a complete fool for weeping like this all the time, at my age."

I was silent.

"There's nothing so foolish as an old fool," she said.

More silence.

"You do think I'm foolish, don't you?" she said.

Many sessions followed in which Jane expressed her conviction that there was something pathetic in her having to pay someone to listen to her problems, sessions in which she repeated over and over again that she was an old fool and it would be better if she could "just shut up."

For some time Jane came regularly but without much noticeable improvement in her emotional state. At times she entered the session in tears, cried throughout the session, and left in tears.

One day while talking somewhat aimlessly in a session, Jane started rummaging through her purse. She was searching for a card, she said.

It seemed that Jane's physician had given several cards for referrals. One was for a bereavement group run by the local hospital.

While fumbling still more in her purse for the other card, Jane asked "What would I do...with all those other people there?" Her expression was one of distaste.

"It's a group for bereavement," I said. "You can hear of how others handle their grief."

"That's sickening," said Jane. "I don't want to hear about other people's troubles, and they don't want to hear about mine." She closed her purse without finding the card.

"If you're looking for foolishness, you could start there," I said.

Eventually Jane did call, and in the first group session she was struck by a revelation that made a great difference in her life. A young woman was talking about the death of her husband and young child in an accident, and Jane suddenly felt the air go out of her. She was literally gasping for breath.

This young woman had loved others with passion, in a way Jane had been afraid to love anyone but her mother, and still the loved ones had been taken from the young woman. Jane wanted to leave, but she couldn't. She listened to the whole of the young woman's story, and then when it was her turn she felt something stirring in her, a reaching out. She cleared her throat and turned to the young woman and said in her gravelly but precise voice "you are braver than I am, young lady. I admire you for it."

In her next session Jane was eager to discuss the young woman, and to speculate on what life might have in store for her now. Jane was also eager to return to the group to hear more of the young woman's story.

In subsequent meetings the group became aware of Jane's preoccupation with the young woman. Several group members expressed interest in hearing Jane's story. When Jane was reluctant, one of the members of the group accused her of being a "voyeur," and Jane was deeply wounded by this remark. But the rest of the group was more patient. Jane's repeated references to the young woman's grief led the group to encourage her not to "put herself down" in comparison to the young woman, and eventually they helped her to give an account of her own grief. The group also encouraged her to realize that her own version of "bravery" had kept her going while alone and isolated for so many years.

In her sessions with me, Jane was edging toward the discovery that she was grieving not for her mother, not for her lost job, but for the lost chances at living which she accumulated "with compound interest," as she put it, over the years. She was beginning to confront the awesome fact that something in her own being had stunted her life. But at this point the inescapable fact of so many wasted years was like a disturbing nightmare that can't quite be remembered, but leaves one shaken nevertheless.

The Ripping Sound of Two Souls Separating

The path now seemed to go through talking about her sainted mother. At the time of her mother's death Jane had no one else to grieve with her. Her mother's death and the grief after it had seemed like an experience uniquely her own, something which no one else but Jane had ever undergone before or since.

Jane had not known that an intense emotion, any very intense passion, can be isolating. Of course this was her own personal grief, but in its gripping power, and in its possibility for all of us, grief was not something that had singled out Jane from among all other humans.

Her grief was real in her "world" but in some way needed to have a frame of reference that allowed for the rest of the world. Like much of her life her grief had a "walled-off" quality that kept her much too separated from the human condition. Becoming more familiar with the human condition, with all of its contingencies, would eventually become a great source of comfort to her.

Her first task was to give voice in the presence of another human being to her violent emotions of grief at her mother's death. As Jane put it in an angry moment:

"If you want to know about this, you will have to hear the ripping sound of my mother's soul being torn from mine."

Session after session of tears and grief and mourning followed. Jane was a person taken over and possessed by grief. Only gradually did it become clear that along with the capacity for carrying and bearing such a grief, there was something vital still alive in her; she still cared about life enough to feel the fierceness of its power. In her wild grief there was a hidden treasure, something that could one day be of great use to her.

As she settled into her new life, Jane accepted part-time work as a records keeper for a small company within walking distance from her home. Her energies were no longer in her work, however. She was faced with the larger task of fashioning for herself a new garment in life, beginning with the first thread of her experience, the thread of her daily grief. Eventually she would need a garment that would fit her as she needed to be, not as the woman who could live only in the lost love of her mother.

A Statement to Eternity and a Problem with Blasphemy

"Why should I start anything new when I'm so close to the end?" Jane asked in a moment of relative calm.

"It seems that your sole criteria for the value of a career or a life, is how much time is left to live it," I said.

"What else is there?" said Jane.

"Good question," I said. "Can you take a stab at it?"

"I wouldn't know where to start."

"What's valuable in your life today?"

"I am looking forward to my bereavement meeting tonight."

"You might start there, with the value of your meetings. What do you get out of them?" Jane had been attending the bereavement group with continued interest.

"They do help me to see things I never saw before. I don't feel as isolated when I'm there."

"Is that a valuable experience...no matter when it happens, with lots or very little time left?"

"Yes, I suppose."

"But...?"

"Well...I'm embarrassed to say it."

Jane gathered herself.

"I want to do something with my life and my career that is eternally valuable. Is that so unreasonable a demand at my age?"

It seemed that at her bereavement group, a visiting speaker had recommended that the participants make a "statement to eternity" with the remaining time left in their lives. This topic had led to weeks of excited discussion in the group. Like the others, Jane was taken with this idea but she was at a loss for what to do about it.

The discussions had also led Jane to her "problem with religion." Since she had been a devoutly religious person up until her first job loss, the lack of a dimension of "eternal values" to her life since then had become very painful to Jane. In particular, the experience of going to church had become intolerable; she simply didn't go anymore. But she had nothing to replace it.

"What is eternity to you?" I asked.

"Why it's something that lasts through all time, isn't it?"

"Anything else?"

"I don't know," she said. "The eternal is so...well, you can't miss it...you'd know it when you see it."

"Yes, it's impressive, among other things. Something that is eternal is very impressive," I said. "This suggests that you aren't sufficiently impressed with what is eternal about your life."

"What do you mean?"

"Well, you said you want your life to be a statement to eternity."

"Yes."

"That entails being impressed with what is eternal about life, day to day...it means not taking such things lightly or dismissing them."

"What am I taking lightly?" asked Jane.

I shrugged, indicating Jane should again "take a stab at it." The session was drawing to a close, and Jane left determined to think long and hard about how she might be "short-changing" the eternal.

But in the sessions that followed Jane had other things on her mind than "what she might be taking lightly" although she did frequently mention her belief that very little of life has any importance unless it reflects something of the eternal. She spent much of the time describing the people and situations that played a role in her life. Many of her sessions were discussions of her feelings of disappointment in how things had turned out, how transitory many things were, and how little true permanence could be found. As she began thinking about old age, she said, life was not what she anticipated it would be, not what she had planned on.

At times during these discussions she took pleasure in describing her old job as if she was still there: the gruff but courtly ex-chairman, the immaculate uniforms of the floor guides with their white gloves, her deep satisfaction at compiling quarterly reports, the thrill of taking her "walk."

At the start of one such session, Jane began again for the uncounted time to repeat her old laments:

"I'm an old fool," she began tearfully. "My life is a complete waste...You're just being kind to listen to me...No one is interested in the troubles of an old lady."

"I can hear the eternal ones crying," I said.

"What did you say?" asked Jane, startled.

"Those things that are eternal...the ones that you are supposed to be dedicating your life to...they are crying about how you've gone astray. You're still worshipping an idol, a false god."

Jane face was incredulous.

"Have you gone mad?" she said. Her mouth stayed open.

"Not at all."

"What on earth can you mean?"

"I mean you're worshipping at the feet of the false god that says if you're old, you're a fool."

"You can't talk to me that way," said Jane.

"Why?" I asked.

"You're supposed to be supportive," said Jane. Tears were pouring down her cheeks. She was shaking. "If I don't have your support, where can I turn?"

"You have my support...but you must recognize by now that this is blasphemy," I said.

"Blasphemy?"

"At this stage in your development, and in your life, it's blasphemy to go on saying these things. You can't be content to think of yourself as nothing but an old fool and at the same time have the hope of serving the eternal values in life."

Jane was silent. "I never thought it mattered that much," she said through her tears.

"So many matters of the soul have serious, even grave consequences," I said.

"Oh, is that what it is," she said. "Yes, I guess it's a matter of whether I'm worth anything."

There was a long silence.

"What can I do about this?" said Jane. "Suddenly I feel guilty."

"Under the circumstances, that could be seen as highly appropriate," I said.

For many more sessions Jane came ready to lament her foolishness, her age, and her wasted years, but each time she did, there was something "in the room," as she put it, which stopped her. In fact she was experiencing her laments colliding head-on with her desire to serve the "eternal values." Here was the collision of two "premises," one old and ingrained, the other newly created. The old premise, that her current life could be spent lamenting the unchangeable past, was incompatible with the new premise of contributing in the present to the highest of life values, to valuing the soul. The emptying of her former attitude to life was nearly complete; now a filling up process could begin.

At the start of a session during this period, Jane was unusually pensive. "There's something new in my life," she said.

I noted to myself that Jane had never used the word "new" before in a positive sense. I felt the fireworks in the room giving off light and heat.

"What's that?" I asked.

"I feel like I've made some progress with 'eternity.'"

"How so?"

"I think I know how I've been shortchanging the eternal. If there is life, it must be lived?"

"Yes."

Jane nodded. "I'd forgotten about that," she said.

Her next few sessions consisted of discussions about the nature of the eternal, particularly those aspects which Jane had excluded from her life. Through these discussions she decided that something eternal is something that can be shared. In one of these sessions she said:

"I can see I made so many mistakes...everything we do is a statement to eternity, isn't it? The important thing is, what statement do you want it to be, don't you think?"

"That's well put," I said.

After a pause, Jane continued:

"There's something very wonderful...when you interact with other people, isn't there?" She paused and tilted her head to the side. "Not always of course," she laughed.

"Yes?" I said.

"If I was taking anything lightly, it might have been how I myself can play a role in the eternal...a role for me...with other people too, don't you think?"

"Could you give me an example?" I asked.

"When I said nobody wants to hear about my grief, I was wrong, wasn't I?"

"Yes, look at how that young woman's life story has opened doors for you."

"I might play that role for someone else, mightn't I?" asked Jane.

"Certainly."

Jane added thoughtfully "It isn't just grief that people might want to hear."

The Pain of Finding a New Way to Worship

After this period of discussion about the eternal and the soul, Jane was noticeably less weepy and depressed. In her sessions she now began talking about two experiences that had also "collided" violently: her isolation and "church."

Jane said the experience of attending church had become painful because there was too much of a gulf between the uplifting moments she often felt in church, moments when she felt in a true communion with other worshippers, and the much greater amount of time she spent alone. She felt a tremendous letdown on Sunday afternoons and evenings, when church was over and she was alone on her sofa. The letdown was sometimes more than she could bear; it caused a pain so great that she avoided going to church altogether.

Weeping freely she said, "I don't know any pain greater than being isolated." This truthful statement, made in great pain but calmly and with strength, indicated that Jane had indeed progressed a long way in her ability to experience things as they really are.

She added "I wish I could go to church without it tearing at me. Why do you suppose I can't?"

"Perhaps it's because you've been under the impression that you can only worship in church," I said.

"What do you mean?"

"Your desire to do something that is eternally meaningful could be compared to the small spark of the divine that's in each of us, the soul. That spark has to be fanned and kept going."

"I don't understand," said Jane.

"An ambition like that takes everything we've got."

"What does that have to do with worshipping?"

"When you pay attention to what's going on in yourself, as you have been doing, then you're also worshipping...when you experience a sense of togetherness with others in your group, then you're also worshipping...All of life is a matter of giving attention to the things we choose to give our attention...we don't have any better name for that than worshipping. As you said, it's a matter of what's being worshipped."

"I have to think about all this," Jane said.

From this time forward, Jane gradually began to show a more workmanlike attitude to the issues in her life; she was now ready to explore the ways in which she had been worshipping a false god, an idol.

It was hard for her to admit that, at her mother's knee, she had learned snobbery and a certain haughtiness. In her role on her old job as a "keeper of the sacred flame" she had been expressing her desire to make work into a worshipping experience, but in a way that proved hollow and distorted. Her previous way of worshipping the company and its "gods," the bosses at work, had been "profane"; it was really serving the "gods" of prestige and one-upmanship. This had led to the emptiness that Jane had to remove from her system, for emptiness takes a major effort to expel.

For many more sessions, Jane shared the intimate details of her life that she had been embarrassed to share with anyone. She brought her aches and pains, her fear of doctors, her dread of smelling bad, her most intimate daily routines. If these were not shared, they could not be worshipped. She expressed her thoughts and feelings, and they became known to her. She bowed her head to the requirements of a more soulful way of living, which at times she found quite objectionable, in particular the collision of her old and new beliefs.

Much of this work had the effect of stripping away Jane's illusions about the devoted attentions of her mother, whose vicarious living through Jane had actually been a terrible burden and had fostered the wasted years in Jane's life. These realizations added a new dimension of sadness to Jane's experience while also helping her to face honestly what she had lived.

It was particularly shocking to Jane to discover that she had clung to her mother's seemingly hidden but nevertheless influential philosophy of life with the assurance that it had been "promised" by her mother to be true. Clinging to the promise, instead of making her own discoveries about life, had kept her from going forward in life. This propensity toward "clinging" was hard to dislodge, it was recalcitrant, and created a great many obstacles that Jane had to encounter.

In a session near an important anniversary of her mother's death Jane was struggling to embrace a new premise:

"What if my life is eternally valuable?" she asked for the uncounted time. Bemused, she added: "Jane's 'world'..." Then she juxtaposed a new thought for the first time: "A crotchety old lady with a sofa problem!" There was incredulity in her voice. After a moment she smiled and laughed.

In the acceptance of these apparent incommensurables, Jane began to embrace a more advanced attitude to life that far exceeded anything she had been exposed to in her corporate and church life. This new development represented a radical departure from her mother's approach to life. It was a proclamation of her own value as "Jane Soul," a special name she started calling herself but just in our sessions. "Jane Soul" was her name for her new identity, living with the eternal interwoven with the mundane--sofa, tears, old age and all. She was discovering what was priceless about having a soul, and that there would also be a price for it:

the threatening fact of getting in touch with the soul is that a former frame of life may have to come crashing down.

For Jane the crash came with the yet liberating discovery about her mother: her mother's essential way of being was to live as if her own soul and her own life were unimportant except to keep up outer appearances. Her mother had "recommended" this attitude to Jane as well, and Jane had adopted it and endorsed it. It took all the effort and time in our sessions together to explore how and why this could be so. It had seemed inconsequential to Jane, but eventually she came to realize that living as if one's life is unimportant is a grave sin, a waste of the gift of life.

In the process, Jane had to suffer the accusation that to think she was important meant she was egotistical and self-centered. Her prejudice, and her mother's prejudice, had been that the desire for importance was something unnatural, something to be "squashed" as she put it. She had never considered that her own inextinguishable desire to be important could be an expression of a precious eternal truth: that the flame of life in her own soul, including her desires and passions, was a priceless treasure. "Of all things I never would have considered this to be the big obstacle. But it makes sense, doesn't it?" she said.

"But what about all those self-important men I worked for so many years?" she asked, her thoughts leaping back once again.

"What about them?"

"They didn't doubt their importance." she said. "They made everyone treat them like they were pashas."

"Was there anything `eternal' about their motivations?" I asked with a smile.

Jane laughed. "Not a thing."

"But perhaps they pretended there was?"

"They made it seem like it was so important." Jane described once again the white gloves of the floor guides, leading visitors to the inner sanctum of the senior executive suite. "They made it seem like church...those pagans!" Jane put her hand over her mouth, awed by what had come out of her.

"My God, I fell for that! For so many years," she said. "How could I

126

be so blind?"

In a new way Jane made the connection that her approach to her work and to church, to life in general, had not been merely influenced, but had been directed by what she now realized was a "pseudo-religion." She had tried to be a worshipful person, to her credit. What she had worshipped had provided her with gainful employment but its hollowness had eventually starved her chances for a full life. She was worshipping a god of appearances and respectability, a god who had no provision for her own individual value. Her multiple job losses offered the "opportunity" to empty out all of her old way of worshipping.

Back to the World

At last, Jane made a momentous decision. She took an evening program on bereavement in the aged. Quite sensibly, she decided that while she might be interested in helping the elderly with their bereavement, she simply was not equipped to handle the process with younger people.

At the end of the course she received a certificate with which she felt encouraged to do volunteer work at a large nursing home. This volunteer position led to a part-time paid position. With her finances in such good order, Jane was finally able to move completely out of her old profession at last.

The part-time nature of the position suited her "just fine," as it allowed for other course work that she had always wanted to pursue including music, philosophy and the arts. There she went through the often stressful but rewarding process of making friends with whom she could laugh, make use of her life experiences, and share her passion for things that mattered. These counterbalances to her work at the nursing home were an essential part of maintaining her equilibrium, and they helped to restore the sense of humor and fun and companionship that were lacking in her years alone.

The problem with her hearing had been a symptom of Jane's problem with attending to and sorting out what should be in the foreground and the background of life. When the part of life that needed to be lived outwardly, in genuine intimacy with others, was in its proper place, and when her private conversations with herself had become a means of clarifying the truth for herself, then the hearing problems dropped away, never to bother her again. She had developed a capacity to hear herself and her own thoughts without having them come at her from the outside.

At the nursing home Jane formed a support group with herself as group facilitator. At last her work was deeply fulfilling. She discovered that her natural graciousness made her a superb hostess, and that the people in the home looked forward to her group as the highlight of their week.

The grief and isolation that Jane lived now became a resource for her work in her new occupation. For, in their intense emotion of grief and, most of the people she encountered were also suffering from isolation.

This common human experience--of grief and isolation--that formerly scared and disgusted Jane, now became a door that she learned how to open to reach others. An entirely new aspect of her personality had been created, a new chamber of the heart, one that reacted with compassion and closeness to the isolation of others. Her interest in other people's thoughts about the "eternal" generated a great stir in the home and made her visits a source of renewed interest in life. As she put it: "For the people at the home there is only one person in their whole week who is honestly pleased to see them. When I say `welcome' they know I mean it. They can't wait for me to get there." She added "And you know I look forward to it as much as they do."

Near her last session, Jane asked: "Could there really be something to admire about me?" Prior to this she had expressed admiration only for others: for her mother, for the young woman facing the loss of her husband and child, for the ex-chairman of the company, for many others in fact but never for herself.

"Go on."

"Mother wanted me to be safe," she said. Nodding, she added "I understand that. That was mother's `church.' It was mine too. I lived a life I thought was safe before but then I came to a dead end. Now I'm living in a way...mother would never have even dreamed of."

"How would you describe that?"

"I'm doing something that no one but me can do...making something from my life...As I understand eternity, that means I will be a part of it..."

As she said this, Jane's gravel-edged voice began to break up, but she sat up straight, smoothed her dress with her hand, and spoke firmly.

"I almost lost my chance...I wasted so much of my life..." Her voice wavered again. Shaking her head up and down she said "Now I know...now I know...what it takes to be a keeper of the sacred flame."

"Yes?" I asked.

Full of emotion, Jane struggled to put her thoughts into words.

"Keeping a pact with what's important in life...that's the pact with the soul...each person is the smallest thing but also the most important..." Smiling through her tears, she added "me, too..." And then she said..."Especially me."

Discussion

Our relationship to our soul can be compared to a "sacred flame" that we have to keep from going out, a flame we have to keep alive by valuing it. The hidden hand of fate in Jane's life was "responsible," if you can call it that, for stripping away the props and supports for a false way of living. First, the supports from her job were taken away, then in our work the confrontation with her mother's values stripped away more illusions, and the final dismantling of her identity and her way of living came with the confrontation with her own distorted values. All this was in service of keeping the "sacred flame" of her relationship to her soul from going out.

We all have the experience again and again that the world can become "too much with us," as Wordsworth put it, and we often realize only after the fact that we have poured our energies into things of unreal importance as if these activities were all that counted. Like many other people, Jane's fundamental life and career premise were originally based on false and unreal assumptions about herself. One of the greatest of these false ideas was that her value as a person could only be derived from the company where she worked. Her story illustrates that shedding illusions of this kind can represent a truly heroic undertaking, and that a seemingly simple act of reflection can be a violent as well as valiant and even epic struggle within one person.

If her soul presented the challenge to experience work as eternally valuable, what could she do about it except pay the price? The price was the emptying out of the unreal, with tears and pain.

Rather than taking us into a realm of retreat and isolation and bitterness, a soulful encounter with our essential path—if followed with integrity to its own genuine destination--brings us back to the world with a new sense of purpose and direction. At all stages of life, keeping a pact with what is important in the career and in life is a daily task to honor a sacred light.

-Chapter Seven-
"I Am a Prisoner of My Job"

Everywhere in the world of work, at every level, there are people who complain that they are "prisoners of the job." This is the story of one man who appeared to have serious limitations of character and temperament -- he described himself as suffering from "emotional locked-in syndrome"-- but nevertheless he overcame a significant part of the experience of being such a prisoner, and began a journey to a form of inner liberation.

Each day Leonard Bregenz dragged himself to his workplace, a small health food shop in Greenwich Village where he stood behind the counter and rang up the purchases of the customers. Tall and thin with a sallow complexion and wispy brown hair, he was a man whose expressionless face and drab appearance seemed to exemplify the word "clerk."

But as much as he might look like one, Leonard was not happy being a clerk. He was continuously irritated by the customers and their earnest, anxious questions about their health and about the store's products. He couldn't care less whether they should take Vitamin C in a buffered form, or whether the dosage of beta-carotene in a multivitamin would be sufficient to prevent cancer.

For Leonard it was torture to listen to them, just as it was torture to stand all day in back of the register, and hand money back and forth. The only pleasure at work for Leonard came during the slow times when he would unload a new shipment of goods and place them in orderly rows on the shelves.

There was something calming about this, something he looked forward to, but naturally it was all spoiled by the appearance of the customers who would mess up the orderliness of the shelves by picking up a bottle of Cod Liver Oil and placing it back on the shelf marked "Latest in Sports Nutrition." It was dismaying to Leonard to watch the customers paw over bottles and then return them with the labels turned the wrong way, away from the front of the shelf.

Leonard often took out his irritation on the customers by making pointed remarks about their slowness at comprehending the store's complicated discount policies or by handing them their change in such a way as to make them fumble with their packages.

Leonard was a bachelor. He described himself as "the son of two alcoholics who couldn't stand a job or each other, drunk or sober." He had learned early in life that the best and safest refuge was "to retire into my room and read." His was an upbringing which was impoverished both emotionally and financially. Interestingly, he neither drank nor smoked, and he did take a comprehensive assortment of vitamins.

He lived alone in a small apartment in a seedy residence hotel near Madison Square Park in the middle of the city. In nice weather, and even sometimes in the cold, he spent much of his free time reading on the benches and watching the goings-on at the park. People were recognizable in their roles and he amused himself by "typing" them: mothers with carriages or strollers, old people with nurses, small children free to run and shout, teenagers with nose rings and purple hair, nefarious types including thieves and drug pushers, foreigners with guidebooks and maps, people who matched their dogs and people who didn't, and of course lovers; all of them were given "names" which Leonard had drawn from literature.

Literature was his primary interest. Leonard took many of the literature courses available at his local "Y." He had an excellent mind for literary facts, as well as facts of any kind; collecting facts produced the same feeling of calm as placing bottles on the shelves. Leonard was an exceptional player at the game of "Trivial Pursuit," but he seldom had anyone to play with.

At the "Y" one evening he heard me speak on the topic of meaning and careers. He called the next week and asked for an appointment.

Leonard began by saying "Something in the talk last week intrigued me."

"What was that?" I asked.

"You said that career problems can arise from loneliness. I'd never heard that before. As a keen observer of human nature, I'm interested to know more about that."

"Are you lonely?" I asked.

"Not particularly," said Leonard. "But I hate my job."

"What do you hate about it?"

"Everything. It's the most maddeningly stupid job anyone could ever have," Leonard said. "I have no interest in anything in it. I am a prisoner of my job."

"Is there something else you would prefer doing?"

"No," said Leonard. He looked defiant.

"I see....tell me more about what you hate about your job."

There was relish, gusto, and even glee in the way Leonard described the tortures of working at the health food shop, everything from the "moronic" shop owner to the "craven" shop manager to the "imbecilic" customers to the "buncombe" and "twaddle" of the claims of some of the health food products. (Again, interestingly Leonard took only the highest quality vitamin supplements himself, based on his extensive research.)

It was apparent that the job was torture for Leonard, but it was equally apparent that he loved hating it. And no matter how much he said he hated it, he never missed a day of work nor failed to carry out instructions. In this regard, he was remarkably pliable. Despite his sarcasm and seeming indifference, or perhaps because of them, he was naively willing to do whatever he was told.

So Leonard was quite willing to take instructions from me. I instructed him to take on small daily assignments which were designed to make his workday more interesting. Of course, as Leonard put it, he was taking on these assignments "only from the observer's point of view, not really as a participant."

The first such assignment was to make a "log" of his moods. Previously he had assumed that all forms of his experience of drudgery were the same. Now he was to use his skill as a "keen observer" to catalogue the quality of the moment of drudgery on awakening, and then to compare it to the moment of drudgery answering the same old questions about vitamins, and to the moment of drudgery standing in line for morning coffee, and to the moment of drudgery at the end of the day when he felt bleak and uncertain in the midst of the crowds rushing on their way home.

This exercise of "mood classification" appealed to the cataloguing and filing instincts which were already on-going sources of satisfaction to Leonard; this was the line of least resistance in his personality. The log exercise served the crucial process of making Leonard aware of what he was feeling. In a small way this meant taking a stance with regard to his moods and feelings, rather than simply letting himself be ruled by them.

It also helped that Leonard used the occasion of the "mood classification" exercise to express his sardonic sense of humor and his not inconsiderable literary imagination.

He began with his morning mood. This he labeled "The Impaled Worm." At the moment of waking he said he felt "like a worm, impaled in its middle by a pin, wriggling with pain and anxiety." This feeling persisted as an undertone throughout his day and was only extinguished with sleep. Not surprisingly, Leonard reported that his digestion was his "weak spot" and that many foods upset him.

The next mood began in the line for coffee at the local deli. He called this "The Soma Conga Line" because it reminded him of the soma takers who anesthetized themselves in Aldous Huxley's Brave New

World. He said that the coffee drinkers were lined up as though they ought to be receiving the elixir of youth, the daily dose of immortality. But instead they were getting a jolt to the nervous system that was just enough to make them remember they were alive. From Leonard's point of view, this meant that they too had prison as their destination.

Leonard noted that the feelings of true drudgery began here, and these heavy burdened feelings forced the feelings of pain and anxiety into the background. Here was his first glimpse of the fact that, independent of his will and previously independent of his own observation, his feelings interacted with each other and modified each other. His moods had a "social organization of labor" among themselves which was quite complex. He was surprised to discover this fully operational system of moods and feelings was not dependent on his conscious awareness.

The mood of irritation at customers he described as both "The Lilliputians Tying Up Gulliver" and "The Princess and the Pea." These were both images for the disturbance of his peace and equilibrium brought on by the arrival of the greedy, impatient and excitable customers. (Much later he added a more hopeful variation on the name for this mood: "The Grain of Sand In The Oyster" which makes the pearl.)

The mood classification process gave him something to look forward to, something was stirred in him by the experience of sorting moods and putting them in their proper place. He actually found himself enjoying the process of cataloging his reactions.

As part of the next exercise, each of the regular customers was assigned a made-up name, a code name, much like Leonard's game in the park. Of course Leonard put lots of energy into picking just the right name, and creating a string of associations and literary allusions to go with it. He was delighted when a woman he had nicknamed "Scarlet O'Hara," because of her dramatic gestures and speech, actually came in one day wearing a Georgia Tech sweatshirt. He began to refer to her as "my peach."

New customers at the store were sorted into types, and when a new customer "broke the mold" and established a new type previously unseen, Leonard found himself excited in the same way as a field biologist who discovers a new species.

One day, for example, he came into his therapy session highly excited because he had found a customer who, while browsing, actually went around the shop putting vitamin bottles back in their proper place. This customer also turned labels back correctly, as if he too were an employee.

"I've labeled him `Homo Correctus' and I've been thinking I should offer him my job," said Leonard dryly. Leonard made sure that this customer received free promotional samples along with all his purchases.

In this way much of Leonard's experience of his work began to undergo a noticeable change. As he put it he was simply "more there," so much so that his boss also noticed the difference and offered him a raise. It was a happier time for Leonard, and without much notice on his part, he started to enjoy going to work.

The work in the therapy began to focus on how the moods interacted with each other. Leonard came to see that part of the "purpose" of the drudgery was to ward off thoughts which gave rise to feelings of anxiety and pain. He realized that he actually courted the feeling of drudgery, in order to dull the edge of his more disturbing feelings. This realization was also exciting to him as an intellectual "proposition." He wrote it down in his log in a special ink which he reserved for "discoveries of major import."

But then after some time had passed he started to become alarmed. What Leonard had only played at, this game of cataloging moods, seemed to have serious consequences. Leonard was edging toward the realization that he himself had been responsible for improving his work situation. He had the dangerous intuition that if he was going to continue in this way, he might change into a new kind of being: an effective person, someone who could truly enjoy his work and his life. The intuition brought with it a looming sense of what terrors might be involved in the death and loss of the prisoner identity.

"The thing I dreaded all along has happened," he said in a somewhat self-mocking tone. "I feel responsible for things. It's worse than being impaled. It's my own designer hell, a prison of my own design." As he pointed out he was now feeling like something of a participant in life, not just an observer. He even bought a new rather sporty wardrobe and got his teeth fixed. The heady elixir of living his own life was starting to get a "bite" into him. But these initial improvements felt ominous to Leonard; he felt unprepared to deal with them.

Leonard now found himself in a state of self-made Purgatory, a tortuous state of suspension, which he compared to Sisyphus pushing the rock up the hill, only to have it fall down again. On the one hand, he had to confront the stark truth that there was a significant part of him which did not want to change, which would prefer to remain miserable, which did not want to "reach out" to the new and potentially rewarding life which he had glimpsed from this seemingly harmless game of cataloging his moods.

On the other hand it was also true that without bargaining for it, he had precipitated a point of "no return" in his life. He was now too much aware of his own capacity for improving his life to return naively to his old way of being. That had been "spoiled" forever. Nor was he prepared to go forward without the most intense reservations.

What followed was a strange new form of misery, different from the misery of his former "drudgery." He was a problem to himself now, where before the problem was his job. If he was moody, irritable and out of sorts, he knew very well that he could get himself out of it by the work of amplifying the mood, classifying it and comparing it, describing it and depicting it. He was no longer "nothing but a prisoner" and he didn't like it.

"Everything before was so familiar," he complained again and again. Leonard had arranged his life in such an orderly way around the prisoner experience. The chaos of his new feelings and the looming possibilities of a new life were awesome burdens he felt unable to deal with.

"I have a right to be miserable," he said with the old defiance.

"That's certainly true," I said.

"Oh God, this is not what I bargained for," Leonard said.

After such a statement he would sink again into a mood of

depression and irritation. But his conscience would bother him and he would arouse himself and begin all over again.

The "rock pushing" Purgatory repeated itself again and again. In this way, Leonard found himself seemingly paralyzed.

After months passed in which he continued with his assignments, Leonard said in a petulant voice: "I would like a vacation from monitoring my moods."

"Say more," I said.

"I'm tired of monitoring my inner experiences. I feel like an air traffic controller, watching a radar screen all day. It's too stressful a job for me. I need a break." Leonard paused. "I'm going to stop for a while and see how I do." Leonard added that he intended to continue his therapy sessions, but would take a holiday from his "mood monitoring" during the week.

After two weeks of his "holiday" he was in great turmoil.

"I can't believe it," he said. The pain on his face was genuine. He looked stricken.

"Believe what?"

"That there could be anything so horrible."

"What is horrible?"

"Every bad mood is assaulting me all at once. I feel like I'm being attacked from all sides, I'm actually under siege. What could cause this all of a sudden?"

"It seems you can't afford a vacation."

Leonard's eyes began to water. "But that's just horrible. It means I'm in a world in which there is no escape." He paused. "You knew about this all along, didn't you?" he said accusingly.

For Leonard the descent from Purgatory into hell had begun. He was realizing that he would never be free of the necessity to monitor his moods. Like eating, sleeping, brushing his teeth and taking a shower, he would have to do "psychic hygiene" every day of his life. Hell was living with the reality that he was a prisoner of this limitation, that it characterized an essentially unchangeable aspect of himself, of life. In the previous period of therapy he had experienced what was changeable about himself and the results had been remarkable and pleasing. Now he was getting to know what was not subject to his whim.

For now, Leonard's main concern was that therapy was not what he had bargained for. Like most people undergoing the process of self-exploration, Leonard had (without being aware of it) set up a number of conditions under which he would undertake the work.

One of these conditions was that when the process became too demanding or uncomfortable, he should be able to take a break. Another condition was that he should be able to decide when his problems ought to fade away. Leonard had the very human but very inaccurate assumption that he should be able to decide, on an arbitrary basis, when he had put in "enough" work on himself.

Even more he felt deceived because he was sure he had received support for this misconception. Up until this point his moods had been largely cooperative; they were changeable through his efforts. But now he wanted the moods to go away altogether, never to return. When they wouldn't, when he began to realize that the responsibility for them would remain as his constant companion, then he rebelled. He wanted to fight this aspect of his fate. In turn the rebellion exacerbated the moods and they were no longer cooperative. They actually started becoming more aggressive. They began to hound him. It seemed like everything he had gained was now lost.

"I don't know if I can go on with this," Leonard said. This time he meant not the mood monitoring but the therapy itself.

"How come?"

"Because it's too painful. I'm not sure I can bear the pain." There was no hint of the old self-mockery in Leonard's voice. "I wanted to get through life without this."

"Without?"

"Without hurting so much." He paused. "This is all getting to me where it hurts."

"What is getting to you?"

"All this," he said. "Life, I guess."

"What does that mean?"

"It means I could always slide by before, pretending it wasn't really me living my life. I could get away from the pain. Now you've led me into the world of inescapable pain."

"If the pain is too much for you to go on, I can certainly respect that," I said.

With tears running down his cheeks, Leonard wrapped his arms around himself and tried to comfort himself. "I'm so much closer now to the pain and the ugliness."

"The ugliness?"

"The ugliness of life. I've been suffering from it since I was a child."

I was silent.

"Life is so very ugly." Leonard stared out the window. "If I didn't get too close to it, I thought I could get by."

"I see."

"I just don't know if I can continue," Leonard said. He got up and walked to the door. "I see now that I am a prisoner of myself, not my job. I can hardly blame my job for things I've carried around in myself since I was a child. That would be naïve, wouldn't it?"

"For sure."

At last Leonard was poised on the brink of a voluntary immersion in the experience of imprisonment, the sine qua non of his building a new life. It was what he dreaded most, but could not avoid. Having brought up to clear view his own role in the experience of being imprisoned, he had already begun to replace involuntary imprisonment with a half-step to voluntary participation in the experience of imprisonment, in the service of something higher. He had brought about the painful "intermediate" stage which awaits all those who genuinely want to overcome the experience of being a prisoner of their job, a prisoner of life.

From this day forward, Leonard began to "drag" himself to therapy, just as he had dragged himself to work. The difficult middle period of therapy had begun, the period in which much of the underlying structure of his personality would be explored, in a fashion he experienced as a "hard slog through slime."

However even though it was a hard slog, Leonard's pleasure in his discoveries continued. For example, he began to see that he had cultivated a facade of "dullness" in social situations to protect himself from the cruelties of the outside world. Dullness was a kind of protective coloration, he said, like that of the leaf-green insects or striped animals who blend in with their surroundings. It was a relief for him to discover that underneath the dull facade, there was much that was interesting about him, if not fascinating.

And during this time he started to confront the issue of his pain directly.

"I told you I've always wanted to get away from what hurts," he said. "I understand all those drug takers in the park. Knowing you are in pain all the time is a dreadful thing," he said. He hastened to add "But now I see that being numb is even worse. That is the worst pain of all." He stared out the window. "I can see that a certain kind of new pain may ensue from the gift of feeling. You know I've always thought of myself as a person with 'emotional' locked-in syndrome."

Here Leonard was referring to the terrible syndrome, a form of nearly total paralysis, in which the body cannot move, except the eyelids, but the mind is alert and aware although locked into an immovable body due to a stroke or an accident. His "emotional" form of the syndrome kept him "locked-in" from life.

"But one thing troubles me," he continued. "What is the meaning and purpose of all this pain? When can it end? What can make it end?"

"Those are important questions," I said. "It's always appropriate to ask the meaning of something."

"I suppose pain is part of the warning system. It's a great motivator too, isn't it?"

"Often," I said. "But not always."

"But I'm still puzzled," said Leonard. "Where does my pain come from? I must confess I have no idea."

Although the source of Leonard's pain was not yet clear, it was certain that it would be beneficial for him to experience the pain as something he could overcome, instead of succumbing. He could make something meaningful from the situation and the predicament even if the meaning of the pain hadn't yielded to his efforts.

Our Talks about Pain

Weeks, months, and then several years passed. Dutifully, Leonard continued to work in the therapy.

"Talk to me about pain," Leonard said. "You seem to know a lot about it."

"What do you want to know?"

"I'm learning there are far more varieties of pain than I would have credited before."

"Yes."

"I've organized my life around trying to avoid pain."

"Yes."

"But not very successfully I've discovered."

"Yes."

"I now see that I must emulate the Count of Monte Cristo. I must get an education while in prison."

Leonard was referring to the main character in the novel by Alexandre Dumas. Edmond Dantès, later to become the Count of Monte Cristo, is betrayed and unjustly imprisoned in the Château d'If. There he is tutored in language, culture and science by a fellow prisoner for eight years before finally escaping.

"I see. Of course you know he was able to get free in the end?" I asked.

"That would be to seek the treasure, would it not?" Leonard replied with a slight smile.

This was good. Leonard's model for his existence as a prisoner now included highly focused learning, and the possibility of the treasure of eventual freedom.

Our discussions of pain became the focus of the therapy. In one of these sessions Leonard asked:

"Must there always be a reason why a person avoids pain? Isn't that a sufficient explanation?"

"It's an infallibly good assumption that something we need to do, but nevertheless conscientiously avoid doing, has a motivation behind it. The simplest motivation is to avoid pain but that's just the beginning of the story."

"Ah, but what is the nature of the story of pain?" Leonard asked.

"In your case much of the pain came from mistakenly experiencing the need to act, to do something about your pain, as coming from the outside as an imposed requirement. That is the pain of being a prisoner, a pain we naturally avoid whenever possible. So often we find we just can't do something when it seems to come from the outside. And that's even and especially if we would benefit so much from doing it."

Leonard nodded and I continued.

"Everything changes when we realize we are acting for ourselves. When we connect to the motivation from the inside, we find ourselves enabled to act. Then we can face the pain of even really difficult situations and facts. When we know we are acting on our own behalf, we are nothing of a prisoner."

"It's your opinion that a lack of inner motivation creates the bars in my prison?" Leonard asked.

"A lack of connection to the inner motivation, yes."

From this point forward, Leonard became an eager learner in our sessions. Once again he made notes in colored inks about his moods, and cross-referenced highly detailed notes about our discussions, and quizzed himself regularly to see if he had integrated the material.

"Why do moods come, or rather why won't they go away?" asked Leonard. "I admit I have much more than a theoretical interest in the question." He added "I really must know."

"Moods come if you haven't made genuine peace with the issue at hand. If you have, then they won't come up because they don't need to come up," I said. "For example, you are called upon to make peace with the fact that your customers are nervous and anxious about their health when they enter your store. In particular that means you have to come to terms with the issues around which you yourself are nervous and anxious. Then you won't be susceptible to a mood of irritation at the customers."

"That has a ring to it," said Leonard. He was thoughtful. "And the mood of despair?" he asked.

"What about it?"

"What is the issue at hand in despair?"

"Can you take a stab at it?"

"No," said Leonard. "At least, not yet," he added.

Each session of therapy was a hammer blow at the stone walls and iron bars of Leonard's prison; first came a hundred, then five hundred, then a thousand blows at the part of his character which kept him from experiencing life as a participant. This steady and persistent effort built up new areas of his personality until they gradually became visible, like a coral atoll rising out of the sea.

After more time in therapy than he had bargained for, the prison sentence seemed to be "up." Like a prisoner whose far-off day of release has surprisingly arrived, Leonard came into a session one day and said simply "I'm ready to go into the most painful thing."

"What is that?"

Leonard's face quivered and he began to tremble.

"Don't you know?" he asked.

"It would be better if you could tell me."

"I'm ugly," he said.

There was a long silence.

"Thank you for not reassuring me," Leonard said.

I nodded. "What does ugly mean to you?"

"It means I can't hope for anything better."

"That could be the epicenter of your pain and your despair," I said. "As well as a hint to its potential resolution."

"What do you mean?"

"Even if we assume that you are ugly, and we dispense for the moment with the reassuring truth about the `eye of the beholder,' where is it written that the ugly don't deserve anything better?"

"I don't know. It just seems obvious...that it's true." Leonard paused. "You don't seem to think so..."

Leonard and I looked at one another without speaking for many minutes. At the end of the session Leonard left without saying another word.

Some time later Leonard came into a session and said in his most formal tone, "I've made a complete review of the relevant literature, and you are correct. Nowhere is it written that the ugly don't deserve anything better. It appears my long-cherished notion is in need of an act of ritual defenestration."

"Yes," I said. "How do you propose to do that?"

"When the time comes, I'll heave it." Then Leonard shook his head back and forth and a look of amazement came across his face. "How did I get this way?" he asked.

"I would say by identifying too much with your surroundings. As you have described, there was much in your early life that was very ugly."

"What would not identifying with my surroundings consist of?"

"Having the sense that the ugliness of your situation was something you could improve upon, something you would work and work to get yourself out of."

"And that, you say, is the epicenter of the pain?"

"The unnecessary pain comes from living a life which doesn't suit you, from accepting the view that there is no hope for anything better."

"There's a recipe for despair," mused Leonard. Then he asked "And what is the necessary pain?"

"Pain that is not of our doing. We all have pain from things we couldn't and can't avoid, things for which we were not responsible. It's necessary to feel that pain because it's real, but we need to put a limit on its meaning. There is no personal meaning to the way you were treated as a child. By that I mean that you did nothing to deserve it. It is a highly regrettable and painful fact that it happened, but its meaning is limited to what effect it had on you. It didn't happen for a reason, or to offer you an opportunity to develop beyond it. It just happened, and most regrettably."

"T'would be a far, far better thing if it hadn't?"

"Without question."

"Are you positing that ugliness has nothing to do with meriting my miseries?"

"Nothing whatsoever."

Leonard was thoughtful. "Yes, I do begin to see the veracity of what you're saying," he said. "The ugliness was a crutch I needed. It's better for a child to think he is imprisoned for ugliness, for anything under the sun actually, than to be imprisoned for no reason at all."

For many more sessions, Leonard worked on identifying the ugly and hopeless things of the past, and differentiating them from his possibilities now. Of course during the entire length of the therapy he had been at work at the process of disidentifying with the ugliness and impoverishment of his upbringing, the experiences which had led him to conclude he was a "prisoner." Now the process was reaching a stage of fulfillment as Leonard was able to grasp that the final step to freedom would be embracing an identity other than that of a prisoner. This great and final step was seemingly simple. As Leonard said it seemed that the most profound and most effective truth of his life could also sound like a cliché: "If you think you're a prisoner, you are a prisoner. And if you don't think you are a prisoner, you aren't."

Without warning Leonard came into a session and said: "I surrender."

"To what?" I asked.

"To myself." Leonard's tone had changed. He was now speaking in a more relaxed way. "I'm not what I thought I was. I thought I was a worm. It turns out I'm a person. It isn't easy for someone who has been living as a worm to move up so far in the phyla, nor is it really fair. But I have no choice. Mutations are part of the evolutionary process. This is one mutation who has no choice of returning to the annelids."

This was Leonard-ese for at least a partial surrender to passion and to life itself. Despite the still pejorative way of referring to himself as a mutation, and the pungent soupçon of helplessness which was still a feature of his attitude to life, nevertheless small but true changes had become apparent over time in Leonard.

He began to see other human beings as "species" in their own right, and as a result a great deal of his rudeness and sarcasm were modified. He no longer woke up every day with a sense of dread. In fact he noted that he now sometimes woke up with a sense of having just made a clever witticism.

He was now willing to discuss whole realms of life--including love-- as possibilities for himself and not just for others. He was also willing to discuss the implications for self-understanding from his idiosyncrasies, including the "typing" of others and the literary allusions into which he had poured so much of his energy. For the first time, he looked at

Gulliver and Job, and the Pea Princess and the Count of Monte Cristo, as more than fellow prisoners in his jail cell.

During the previous years nothing much had happened in Leonard's career and his living arrangements. Now when his boss offered once again to send him to a seminar on salesmanship, Leonard finally accepted. At the seminar Leonard met a girl who seemed appealing. They began to date. As might be expected, Leonard suddenly found himself ambitious to have a more suitable apartment.

He mailed a finely crafted letter to a contact at a large chain of furniture stores, asking for information on management positions. The letter brought him an interview and then a job offer at a much higher salary. He gave notice at his old job.

In his last two weeks at the health food shop, he made a special effort to say good-bye to all his regular customers. The parting was difficult for Leonard, he felt like he was leaving his "creations" behind.

"Someone else will have to care for them," he said. "And I did care for them, didn't I?" Far from an irritant, they now seemed like something dear, these "creations." For some time now, Leonard had solicitously made sure that each of his regular customers was aware of the latest literature on vitamins and antioxidants. He had become something of a trusted "consultant" for many of the customers, guiding them into use of the best quality supplements. He was touched more than he would have expected when several of the customers brought him farewell cards during his last week.

At this point, Leonard had not surrendered completely. He was holding out reservations about how much he would surrender to life, to joy and happiness. By some standards, Leonard's oddness would still have led some to label him by any one of several psychiatric categories. But nevertheless he was doing a creditable job with his life, as much as was within his means.

And the "surrender experience" became a powerful source of reference for Leonard. He not only surrendered many of the negatives of his life: the drudgery, sarcasm and rudeness. He also surrendered to many of the good things of life, to satisfying companionship with "Lady

Godiva" as he called his girlfriend, to the heady experience of being a successful business "executive" with an office door which he could close when he wanted privacy, and to the delight of having a spacious new apartment with a doorman he called Sancho Panza, the squire of Don Quixote.

Within his own orbit, and within his own abilities, Leonard had fashioned a place of birth from his old prison.

In the last few sessions of his therapy, there was a topic which was of primary interest to Leonard:

"I'm still asking myself what is the metaphor I'm living by, the one to replace being a prisoner. I'll always be an ex-prisoner in some way, but that's not enough of a metaphor," he said. "It hardly does justice to me now that I've taken a breath of freedom."

"What have you been considering?" I asked.

"For the time being," he continued, "I've settled for one. I believe I'm primarily a pure research scientist when it comes to life. I have a decided fondness for investigation and discovery and I even have an interest in their applications. But I've been concerned because as a research scientist I might not be much of a profiteer."

This was Leonard-ese for his remaining doubts about how much satisfaction and happiness he could wring from life. Brightening, he added "But I do have an interest in patents. All discoveries I make are under my own patent. And if patented, I can profit from them and get some of the benefits from them, and that's more than enough to live on for now."

Listening to Leonard, I saw those fireworks once again, the fireworks that celebrate transformation in a human being.

He had a final comment to make.

"When I first came here I was living under a great deception."

"Yes?"

"I am not free to be anyone but me."

"Yes."

"I had conceived the idea that was a prison."

"And?"

"Now I am free to choose something about which I have no choice."

Discussion of "Prison"

It's not just people with Leonard's bounded limitations of character who experience their job as a prison. For many people from all walks of life, the first appearance of the requirement, from within oneself, to serve something greater is very often experienced as an imprisonment. The dawning of this realization usually comes gradually and then as a big disturbance, a real whopper of a shock. We are no longer free to imagine we are entirely free. The collapse of this illusion is extraordinarily painful, especially when the illusion has been practically an entire basis for living. As Leonard learned, this illusion leads to "escape hatch" living, which expresses itself in the belief that we can devise ways to escape from fundamental aspects of ourselves.

But what are those fundamental aspects and how can we be sure we know what they are? Leonard thought his pain, and his complete domination by his moods, were fundamental aspects of himself—they seemed immutable and therefore fundamental. But he was wrong. The pain greatly lessened and the moods did too.

What was fundamental turned out to be an inner requirement to experience himself as a maker of choice. This was a bigger job than he thought he could tackle. But when he did, naturally he got a bigger outer job too. There are no guarantees that things will work out that way, but nevertheless they often do.

We say that a prisoner is "taken." The experience of being taken as a prisoner is of course objectionable. But that is not all there is to being taken. In a voluntary relationship of love, one or both of the partners will often say "I'm taken." In the stories in this book we have seen many ways in which we are also "taken" by the necessity to follow our inner guidelines and to honor something greater in ourselves that comes to us as a given. Being taken can be a misery or a joy.

From the inside, the most powerful prison anyone can experience is the prison of the wrong premise and the wrong attitude towards life. Living without a connection to our inner dimensions makes us a bystander or observer to our own life, anything but a full participant. By contrast, the feeling of being a participant in one's own life is inherently meaningful and satisfying; it produces still more passion and energy in a kind of round robin of "continuous improvement" in the experience of life. In the same way, the feeling of not being the inhabitant of one's life drains off energy progressively and spirals the experience of life downward. As far as meaning goes, the stark fact is that the rich get richer and the poor get poorer.

What are the chief obstacles on the path to real liberation, to the experience of the attitude of full participation in one's own life, to the feeling that "I'm living the life I was meant to live?" It seems that among the most liberating yet difficult facts to grasp and to accept is the fact that some early difficulties and suffering may not have been necessary or inevitable. As children, many of us form the premise that we are responsible, in some deep and essential part of us, for the conditions and events of our early environment. It can be a huge release to grasp that these conditions may have been an accident of fate. To be sure, everyone is challenged with understanding the extremely important effects of these happenstances, including the ways in which we may now perpetuate the ill effects ourselves. But it is a relief beyond measure to discover we did not have a responsibility for their origin. This realization opens up a whole new world of self-acceptance. Without an acceptance of the truly accidental nature of many elements of fate, the meaning of life cannot go forward because the burden of responsibility is improperly placed. As a major life task, sent by the soul, each of us has to sort out meaning and meaninglessness.

This fact seems like a paradox at first. But sorting out what is meaningful and what isn't, what is truly unchangeable and what is ours to change, makes for the difference between a free soul and an imprisoned one. Liberation doesn't mean being liberated from limits—a goal none of us can achieve. Instead, liberation involves freeing the meaning of the limits. It's truly inspiring that even a person who starts out badly in life can, under the right conditions, transform the butterfly of the soul.

Thoughts

-Chapter Eight-
Every Profession Has an "Antique" Soul or Sacred Premise.

I would like now to reverse the direction of the stories. There the emphasis was on finding meaning from within, from the most personal and individual dimensions of the human soul. Now I would like to address the questions: what does the outer world have to say to our inner world? Where is the soul in the workplace?

To begin, I would like to explore a proposition: Every profession has a sacred premise or "antique" soul.

Each and every profession has a core essence with highly particular qualities, and these qualities tie back energetically to its ancestral (as well as modern) reason for being. This fact is exceptionally important because it gives us all the possibility of experiencing our work as part of something greater--the meaningful enterprise of mankind's journey as a whole.

In fact when we connect to the antique soul of our profession, we can experience a kind of deep meaning for which there is no substitute. This "hook-up" to meaning makes all the difficulties of daily living bearable, and allows us to feel a sense of purpose and rightness about our work and profession. The stronger our connection to the antique soul of our profession, the more we can create within it (and the more we can withstand whatever soullessness may exist around us).

Like the energy in the ground in the form of oil or gas that must be tapped (which takes work!) in order to be used, there is a pool of energy in the antique soul of a profession that needs our conscious awareness (and often further conscious awareness) in order to be reached, tapped, refined and used to power up our lives.

In order to grasp how there is an antique soul with a sacred premise behind a profession, we have to look first at the profession without reference to its current practitioners. For example, it may be true that lawyers in our era have a poor reputation among the professions, and for very good reasons. But this lamentable state of affairs will only distract us from searching out an understanding of the antique soul of the legal profession. Instead we have to ask the question, "In its core essence, what is the legal profession supposed to do?" From an objective perspective, and without judgments based on its current practitioners, what does the profession of the Law set out to accomplish for human beings, in a timeless way? This may be called the "antique soul" of a profession.

The sacred premise or antique soul of the Law is that there must be boundaries and limits on what can and cannot be done. There must be boundaries because we can't live with chaos. The Law set outs the way we need to live among each other, as people who live in societies and civilizations.

The premise behind the Librarian is that he or she is the keeper of the sacred flame of knowledge, the one who is responsible for the continuity of learning and the treasured legacy of the accumulated findings of the people of the present and the past.

The premise behind the Journalist is that the facts need to be known, just as they are. The journalist may be hoping that no one was hurt in an accident, but he or she must report the facts exactly as they happened. The sacred obligation to the facts is the premise that underlies this profession. A journalist asked me "Isn't the sacred premise of my profession to tell Truth to Power?" You can't tell truth to power or undertake any other journalistic enterprise until you know the facts first.

The soul premise that supports the Teacher is that while certain aspects of knowledge may be learned on one's own, nevertheless we all need to have learning transmitted to us by others. The Teacher ensures the continuity of the traditions of our human "tribe" by mediating the knowledge to those who are learning. (Socrates called it acting as a "midwife.")

The premise behind the Salesperson is that products must be made known to those who can use them. For the most part, markets don't reach out to customers by themselves—there have to be Salespeople to introduce the benefits and services to others. The dimension of the sacred premise here is that very little could be exchanged, very little that humankind produces or creates could be made use of, without the Salesperson.

The premise behind the Banker is that the energy of human work must be stored in some fashion, and released when expenditures are required. Banking could be compared to the function of the adrenal glands in the body, which release stored up energy into circulation through adrenaline when action is required. The premise that underlies the Banker is that only when resources are heaped up and accumulated with something in reserve do they allow us to make choices freely later on.

The sacred premise behind the Actor is that by mastering his or her art and craft, the actor leads the audience to participate (through identification) in new experiences, to experience new feelings, and to think new thoughts. Knowingly or unknowingly, the Actor draws on the ancient art of the shaman, who was able to use the underlying dramatic structure of life to lead the people to a new experience by vividly engaging their imagination. When an Actor portrays grief or pity or realization or happiness, he or she draws on the sacred premise that a new pattern and new meaning can be understood and experienced by the audience, when shown in the right way.

The sacred premise of the fashion industry begins with the fact that we all feel enormously different in different clothing. (Everyone has had the experience of feeling attractive and full of life in a favorite outfit, while feeling uncomfortable and unlike "oneself" in another.) Colors, fabric, and styles affect us in ways that are astonishingly varied and highly specific to each of us. The sacred premise underlying the fashion industry is that we all need our clothing to work with us in expressing ourselves, whether in dressing up for a formal occasion, for work, for relaxation and leisure, or dressing for the outdoors.

New professions have an "antique soul" or sacred premise just as much as any others. The sacred premise of the Computer Programmer is that the underlying code that makes up human knowledge can be applied to make things run. By learning and using the properties of symbols, mathematics and language, the Programmer's instructions create a new path on which applied knowledge can flow.

A controversial and very powerful implication of these ideas is that no profession is inherently more sacred than another, including the priestly professions! The overall essence of work is that all professions participate in the sacred dimension of life and all professions have a soul. The person who honors the sacred premise of their profession is living a soulful life—we all get a sense of that kind of person when we meet them, as we do in every walk of life.

But it's often very hard for people to find a balanced way of living in connection with the sacred premise of their profession. The deeper meaning becomes ours, and rightfully so, if and only if we serve the sacred premise of our profession. The renewing energy from the big barrel or keg of energy stored up in the "antique" background of our profession is ours only if we serve the profession's antique soul.

It's a mystery that only some of us need to have a sense of a higher purpose that helps to inform and direct the daily practices of our work. Serving the sacred premise of a profession gives a pay-off of a profound sense of living a life worth living.

However we are always in danger of reversing that process, i.e. trying to get that sacred premise to serve us in inappropriate ways. We are always in danger of misusing the antique soul of our work. The journalist who bends the facts, the lawyer who disrespects the needs of justice, the salesman who preys on the fears of his clients, the programmer who doesn't test his code—these are all examples of the ways in which we can betray the sacred premise of our profession.

The world of work is full of people and situations that defile and

159

debase the sacred premise of a profession, and disparage the soul values of the workplace. For example, the profession of banking has nearly unhinged itself from its sacred premise, to the detriment of society at large and to the detriment of those who are its workers.

Nor do the problems stop there. We are all too familiar with the person who overdoes their identification with the sacred function of their profession. In Jungian language, this is the person who identifies with the persona of their profession. Many of us have known the caricature of the Librarian whose stuffy presence serves to intimidate the patrons of the library from using the materials ("I am the keeper of the sacred flame, and who are you to make inquiries?") rather than encouraging library patrons to learn how to use the resources.

Then there is the Teacher who has "burned out" and is going through the motions of imparting knowledge. Rather than embodying the premise of his or her profession, this person embodies its opposite, a profane premise. One such teacher told me, "I don't learn anything from my students."

And cynical people in all professions channel their own disappointments into the chorus of meaninglessness that threatens the morale of many a workplace ("Who are you kidding? There's nothing sacred about this crummy old job.") ("The most annoying people are the customers.")

These examples show that the betrayal of the sacred premise of a profession can occur in myriad ways, and can sneak up on us without our awareness or consent. It's not easy to come to the realization that

Work inherently makes a continuous claim on us, a claim on our attitude of service to the soul.

What does that mean: work has a claim over us? The very idea almost seems like an affront to our freedom and autonomy. It could lead us to the experience of being a "prisoner" of our job! Yet the moment we step into work of any kind, any profession at all whether taxi driver or middle manager or artist, we have moved into a territory where claims of a complicated nature are invisibly made upon us. Every profession has a remarkably powerful field of requirements, including a whole constellation of essential factors that operate on us--both in the most practical of matters and at the same time at the level of the soul. This set of irreducible dynamics and inescapable conditions begins with the practical matters of getting a license or a company identification badge, or a desk and business cards, or a set of paints as an artist. But then we are immediately "asked" by our life and our work to find an answer to the equally essential matter of how are we going to dedicate our work and our work attitudes to serving the core essence of profession, its raison d'être.

When we bow to the specific claims of our work, and its soul-level requirements, we have a chance for an experience of meaning that is often far deeper and more profound than many people would believe possible. On the other hand, ignoring these "soul" claims produces an equally complicated set of symptoms including boredom and restlessness, illness, fear, anxiety, discouragement and depression. These symptoms and their suffering indicate we have not realized that we have to "pay" something to our profession, a payment that amounts to a "debt."

For example, the taxi driver who drives carefully, knowing that both he and his passengers are precious cargo, is ennobled by serving his profession. If he develops an expertise on traffic flow at certain hours, and a mental picture of where back-ups and danger are likely to occur, then he brings to his work something more than his passengers are often aware is in operation. This taxi driver can go home at night with a sense of pride in his work, having skillfully maneuvered the streets of the city on behalf of his profession and his fellow man. Let no one look down on his work, at the risk of injuring the sacred premise of work itself. The taxi driver may be content in this profession and have a sense of its suitability for him, while yet having urgent dreams of doing other work. In either case, what comes next in his career will frequently hinge on whether he can conduct his work today in a fashion that honors the highly specific context of his work.

On the other hand, if he adopts a conventional attitude of false hierarchies, a view that demeans and disparages his work, a false premise that pictures his work as in some way inferior or unworthy or unimportant, then he will be sullen, curt, and depressed. He will most likely experience the all-too-common feeling of being "stuck" in his profession, an experience that settles on people in every profession and at every level of education, salary and personal background. Above all, he will be unable to find his individual path, precisely because he has accepted a non-individual (i.e. collective or generalized) attitude about what a career should be, and how it should be experienced.

This "continuous soul-claim" dimension of work makes a similar claim within all other professions. For example there is the financial advisor who carefully steers her clients to the investments that are suitable for them, while alerting the clients to where the dangers and "potholes" are likely to be. She will go home at night with a sense of having maneuvered the "street" on behalf of her clients and she will rightfully have pride in her work. Conversely, if she accepts an attitude endorsed by some these days, that helping people with money matters is a profession devoid of meaning, then she will become…sullen, curt and depressed. She will be paying the claim on a distorted view of her profession's premise.

Taking a look at the state of work generally in our culture, we can see that the importance of these highly individual work contexts, and their claims on us have been "injured" in our era. The claims of work over us have been ignored and dishonored, and a one-sided view of work has damaged our collective ability to experience work as truly fulfilling. My view, shared by many others, is that the longer and longer working hours of the average American are a direct result of this injury: as if meaning in work could be found solely in working more hours.

The idea that we have something larger than ourselves to serve in our profession—whatever it is!--is part of what has been lost in regard to work, and part of what has caused the harm to the concept of work. Many aspects of work that require an important place in our careers, but not the central place, such as making money or achieving recognition, have displaced the central sacred premise of work. A one-sided focus on any single element interferes with serving the soul requirement of our work.

Essentially our culture has misread the purpose of work. Renewed attention to the purpose of work can reclaim the meaning of work.

This misapplication of the purpose of work has enormous consequences. In such a culture as ours, many people can find no path to the soul in work. That is a cause of truly profound suffering. In the case of far too many people, there is a need, solely for the sake of survival, to feign agreement with the "unreal importances" of so much of what our culture produces. Much of our culture is unreal and the workplace seems to grow more unreal more rapidly.

In the midst of this parlous state of affairs, it is a source of comfort and solace to me, and I hope to the reader, that the "repair" work for this injury can be done, even in the midst of a culture-wide misreading of the purpose of work, by each individual through their own encounter with themselves--even in an era when so many people have lost the connection to the meaning of work and career meaning. The process requires consistency and discipline and dedication; it is up to each person to determine whether the application of these energies is worth the effort.

Of course personal fulfillment is what makes the effort worth considering. But it's equally important to emphasize the importance of how honoring the antique soul of our profession also connects us to others. One of the great rewards of devoting oneself to the sacred premise of work is that we are then in a position to find others who complement our own nature, and our own devotion. This organic connection to other people who share a commitment to the core principles of a profession is a unifying factor in life, one that connects us in spirit to others no matter what they do. Connecting to others with the same spirit is nothing to be underestimated! Respect for one's work leads to respect for oneself as well as for others and is a powerful antidote to isolation and meaninglessness. The spirit of dedication to a higher principle at work also connects people across the professions; such an attitude connects the dedicated nurse, salesman, fireman, taxi driver, attorney, and programmer in an inclusive circle.

From all of this we can conclude that it is a lifelong task to honor the soul of our profession. At each phase and stage of our work, we must become aware of new tasks that await us in order to fulfill this requirement from our occupation. Every day, week and year of our lives is a demonstrated answer to the question "How are you living in relation to the deeper meaning of your work?"

For each of us, there are unique tasks in this regard that arise from the specific nature of our work and our attitudes toward what we do. But at the most general level, all of these tasks may be summarized in a single idea.

The soulful purpose that all occupations and professions share is to serve the process of creating something new.

When we work, we are meant to be creators. When we work, we participate in a new daily rite or ceremony of creation that is inherently satisfying and meaningful if only we can tune in to this dimension of our life. If we have problems experiencing ourselves as creators at work, it's not the sacred dimension of our occupation that is lacking. Instead it's our own lack of development when it comes to serving the sacred nature of work. With such a realization, we are "sent" back to work on ourselves, to improve our ability and capacity to be an instrument of the deeper meaning of work.

-Acknowledgments-

The ideas in this book are based on the work of C.G. Jung. Readers who would like to know more about Jung's ideas can find an amazingly rich source of jewels in his Collected Works, and in the works of Marie-Louise Von Franz.

I am deeply grateful to the late Yoram Kaufmann, to whom this book is dedicated. Dr. Kaufmann's pioneering book, The Way of the Image, The Orientational Approach to the Psyche, crystallized Jung's ideas and is essential reading for anyone who wants to know more about the human psyche.

The following dear friends and colleagues read this book in manuscript and gave very helpful feedback. Many thanks to: Ayda Akbelen, Mim Anzolut, Judith and David Bess, Brian Blake, Karen Bridbord, David Brooks, Deborah E. Brown, Haig Chahinian, Dan Coben, Chris D'Amico, Steve Davis, Robert Evanila, Meredith Gardner, Harriet Gluckman, Dr. Erik Goodwyn, the late George Hahn, Kereena Hewitt, Aisha Holder, Lola Holness, Anita Lands, Joan McGovern, Margaret Maguire, Hemda Mizrahi, Fran Parker, Karen Rancourt, Neil Rindlaub, and Deborah Ziegler. Special thanks for a very close reading of the manuscript to Randy Place.

Thanks to Sheryl and David Spanier for insightful feedback and advice, and for extraordinary friendship over many years.

Jean Sun Shaw read the manuscript in its earliest and latest versions and gave invaluable support and feedback.

Thanks to Jenny Moore and Lloyd Clunie for the beauty of warm friendship.

Thanks to John Teton, lifelong friend and founder of the International Food Security Treaty.

Thanks for long friendship to Doug Freeman, Ira Glasser, Andrew Sacks, Marc Silverman, and Rob Womack.

Thank you to Fred Ciporen for soul to soul friendship.

If I have omitted anyone to whom I owe acknowledgement, please contact me.

I am very grateful to Janet Careswell, Executive Director of the C.G. Jung Foundation of New York for years of fruitful work together.

Thanks to my step-daughters, Naama Laufer-Correia and Maayan Laufer-Murdoch and their husbands, Luis Correia and Rodrigo Lopresti, for love and friendship. Maayan is the designer of this book's cover and a valued guide to the publishing process. To our Leah Laufer-Correia, besos and beijos.

Benette Rottman has been both a loved and treasured sister and a friend.

Thanks to Natasha LeTanneur for love, creative inspiration and ideas, and for being my wonderful daughter. Thanks to my wife, Hannah Laufer-Rottman, for love, partnership and a soul connection beyond words. Toda raba mi amore.

-About The Author-

David Rottman is Past President and Chairman of the Board of the C.G. Jung Foundation of New York. He is a member of the Continuing Education Faculty of the Jung Foundation and has taught courses on Jungian Psychology for more than 30 years. He lives and practices in New York City.

To Contact the Author

You may contact the author at david@davidrottman.com

Made in United States
North Haven, CT
08 March 2022

16911185R00102